A Call to Unity, Peace, and Purity

A Call to Unity, Peace, and Purity

Post-Denominationalism, Reconciliation, and the Reclamation of the Christian Faith

STEVEN W. WILLIAMS

WIPF & STOCK · Eugene, Oregon

A CALL TO UNITY, PEACE, AND PURITY
Post-Denominationalism, Reconciliation, and the Reclamation of the Christian Faith

Copyright © 2026 Steven W. Williams. All rights reserved. Except for brief quotations in critical publications or reviews, no part of this book may be reproduced in any manner without prior written permission from the publisher. Write: Permissions, Wipf and Stock Publishers, 199 W. 8th Ave., Suite 3, Eugene, OR 97401.

Wipf & Stock
An Imprint of Wipf and Stock Publishers
199 W. 8th Ave., Suite 3
Eugene, OR 97401

www.wipfandstock.com

PAPERBACK ISBN: 979-8-3852-6461-2
HARDCOVER ISBN: 979-8-3852-6462-9
EBOOK ISBN: 979-8-3852-6463-6

01/06/26

Scripture quotations are from the ESV® Bible (The Holy Bible, English Standard Version®), © 2001 by Crossway, a publishing ministry of Good News Publishers. ESV Text Edition: 2025. The ESV text may not be quoted in any publication made available to the public by a Creative Commons license. The ESV may not be translated in whole or in part into any other language. Used by permission. All rights reserved.

This manifesto is dedicated to my entire family, which has faithfully been an encouragement to me whatever the season, and in honor and remembrance of all our family throughout the generations who have sacrificed so much to reconcile the church and reclaim the Christian faith from the Christian religion in the blessed inheritance that we all share in Christ (1 Pet 1:3–5).

I would like to extend my grateful appreciation to James B. Hurley, DPhil, PhD, professor emeritus at Reformed Theological Seminary, and to Jerry Newcombe, DMin, executive director of Providence Forum, for their timely contribution in providing constructive advice and direction regarding this project.

Contents

Author's Note | ix

Prologue | xix

Section 1. Where Did It All Begin? | 1

Section 2. The Age-Old Problem: The "Garden Problem" | 12

Section 3. A Bit of Background: Why Has the Church Been So Divided? | 29

Section 4. Hope for the Church: Returning to the Scene of the Crime | 50

Endnotes | 87

Concluding Remarks: The Christian Faith vs. the Christian Religion | 89

Epilogue | 91

Appendix A: Criticisms | 93

Appendix B: Common Depictions of Christianity | 96

Appendix C: Thinking Outside the Box | 98

Appendix D: The Concept of a "Multiverse" | 100

Appendix E: Community Fellowships of Christ's Church | 105

Appendix F: Example of a Statement of Faith | 107

CONTENTS

Appendix G: Example of a Post-Denominational Church | 110
Appendix H: Establishing a Post-Denominational Church | 115
Bibliography | 117

Author's Note

WHEN I FIRST EMBARKED on this journey, I intended to write a treatise—a formal exploration of a single subject. However, as my pursuit deepened, I realized I was crafting a manifesto: a declaration and a call to action. Unapologetically, this has become my burning passion—a fire that only grows with time—to see the church restored to unity, peace, and purity.

Throughout this pilgrimage, I have discovered that the only viable hope lies in God's people rising above man-made traditions and embracing his revelation as wholly sufficient for the Christian life, regardless of time or culture. If God had given us only a fragment of the knowledge necessary for this, leaving the rest for us to discern on our own, then what would be the point? This would not make sense in that this would only encourage human beings to devise and set forth their own "authority" vis-à-vis God's revelation.

It is essential to recognize that God intentionally provided sufficient knowledge to counter any claim by individuals or communities to speak with authority equal to his. To allow otherwise would be to endorse humanism—an unyielding adversary of God in this fallen world. Humanism is fundamentally a worldview asserting that truth originates from human experience, expressed through two primary forms: philosophy and religion. As I will explore in greater detail later, both serve as Satan's typical modus operandi as counterfeits to God's revelation, captivating humanity

Author's Note

and fostering a false sense of identity and security. This dual expression is often categorized as either philosophical or secular humanism or sacred or religious humanism.

Understandably, any critique of philosophy and religion may provoke defensive reactions, especially from those well-versed in these disciplines. Such individuals may dismiss these concerns as narrow-minded or rooted in an overly simplistic worldview. However, a deeper reflection on the purpose of God's revelation reveals the need for a robust apologetic against humanism.

This manifesto is not intended to discourage education in philosophy or religion. Instead, it emphasizes that neither is the foundation for understanding the Christian faith. Historically, philosophers and religionists—often including Christian theologians and clerics—have, in their zeal to advocate for their causes, contributed more to division than to promoting unity, peace, or purity. In this manifesto, my focus is on religion, which has been the primary means of deceiving God's people throughout history. Religion, originating from humanity, seeks to understand, explain, or experience God and the spiritual realm through human effort rather than relying on God's revelation. Ultimately, religion is Satan's counterfeit, transforming the genuine faith of God's people into a human-orientated system.

As many of us were taught as children, Christianity is often presented as one among many religions from which one might choose. The popular Latin phrase *In necessariis unitas, in dubiis libertas, in omnibus caritas* (In essentials unity, in nonessentials liberty, in all things charity)[1] has in times past been invoked to navigate religious conflict. Yet, it continues to be a fruitless task to find agreement on what constitutes "essentials" versus "nonessentials."

While growing up in my family, we were taught to respect all people and to avoid speaking negatively about other religions. Privately, however, we held that Christianity was the best of all religions. Later, in theological circles, I encountered arguments defending Christianity as the "true religion," quoting esteemed figures such as John Calvin in his *Institutes of the Christian Religion*

---

1. Wikipedia, "In necessariis unitas."

Author's Note

or Jonathan Edwards in *Religious Affections*. Even Jesus, it was argued, participated in the religious practices of Judaism. Religion seemed inseparable from the Christian tradition, deeply embedded in our minds and culture.

It wasn't until much later that I began to understand more accurately what "religion" truly entails, despite its historical usage among Christians. The realization dawned on me like a sudden epiphany: my previous efforts to defend the Christian religion had been misguided. What began as the simple faith of God's people had, by the second century CE, gradually become institutionalized and "religionized"—a transformation driven by well-meaning but ultimately misguided church leaders.

This realization brought me sorrow. What once felt like a justified defense of Christianity now felt like a tragic misunderstanding. To my surprise, I found myself agreeing with the criticisms of religion often voiced by narrow-minded fundamentalists whom I had previously dismissed. While my perspective may differ from theirs, I now sympathize with their complaints and even share common ground with the so-called "nones" and others who criticize religion for its role in much of the world's strife.

Satan often uses religion to deceive the church, exploiting its appeal to our spiritual instincts. Religion encourages us to view the church as a human institution, governed by worldly structures and rules, rather than as an organic family led by God-ordained leadership. It exalts individuals with a reputation for being religious instead of fostering singular devotion to God. Religion seduces us with rituals, impressive buildings, and worldly trends, diverting our senses from the truth revealed in God's word. Ultimately, religion is humanity's distortion of the Christian faith—a counterfeit orchestrated by Satan.

From the beginning, Satan has attacked God's word, as seen in the garden of Eden's question: "Did God actually say?" (Gen 3:1). This pattern persists today, whether through liberal reinterpretations that conform to culture or legalistic additions that claim Scripture is insufficient. Both approaches undermine trust in God's

Author's Note

revelation, replacing it with human constructs and corrupting the true faith with religious humanism.

We are living in the latter days, witnessing increasing ungodliness in the world and a growing divide between true believers and nominal Christians. One unprecedented example of this decay is the attack on humanity as God's image-bearers, specifically in the rejection of binary distinctions of male and female. Such a blurring of God's design is a profound fundamental distortion of his creation never encountered in the past.

Scripture warns of a great delusion leading people away from truth (2 Thess 2:11), and Christ foretold that even believers would face deception (Matt 24:24). At the heart of this delusion lies humanism, both philosophical and religious, which threatens those who identify as Christian yet remain captive to a counterfeit faith.

Historically, I see the Christian church as passing through four great CE epochs: 1) first through fifth centuries: the foundational years of Christian theism and the encroachment of Christian humanism; 2) sixth through fifteenth centuries: institutionalism and the medieval church; 3) sixteenth through twentieth centuries: reformation and the rise of denominationalism; and 4) twenty-first century and beyond: post-denominationalism, reconciliation, and the reclamation of the Christian faith. Each epoch has and will have both hopeful as well as challenging forces to encounter.

The good news is that today Christ is reclaiming his church, uniting true believers in faith and truth while exposing the divisive doctrines of man-made religion. It is imperative that Christians align themselves with God's revelation rather than human traditions, as history will ultimately vindicate those who stand on his word.

In this manifesto, I will lay out indictments against much of organized Christianity. While this will undoubtedly provoke anger or dismissal among many, there will, however, be a remnant who will increasingly acknowledge these arguments as common sense. Too often, theologians and clerics have focused on preserving their reputations rather than addressing the practical needs of the church. Many believers, weary of denominational divisions and

Author's Note

institutionalized religion, have become "dones"—walking away from the organized church—or "nons," embracing non-denominational faith. My goal is to foster a more promising future by suggesting that our Lord is now guiding his church forward toward a more mature post-denominational body of believers who will be a stronger witness for his glory in a troubled world.

The Protestant world, like Roman Catholic, Eastern Orthodox, and Oriental churches, faces significant challenges in retaining believers. Mainline liberal churches have hemorrhaged members, and even committed evangelicals are losing patience with traditions and denominations. While denominationalism once served as an effort to correct past errors, the future may lie in a post-denominational Christian faith—a reclamation of the faith and reconciliation of the church. After half a millennium and over forty thousand denominations, could the church dare to hope for a future beyond these divisions? A new expression may emerge, not as a "restoration movement" attempting to merely recast first-century Christianity, but as a purified community united in faith, free from the constraints of religion, and reconciled to Christ's vision for his church.

In this struggle, there are generally three people groups. There are those who are: 1) traditionalists/denominationalists—those who stubbornly refuse to move beyond the status quo by placing their significance and security in their particular tradition, denomination, or movement; 2) non-denominationalists—those who cast stones at the traditionalists/denominationalists, blaming them for the scandal of division while retreating into their own autonomous and unaccountable corners of safety; and 3) post-denominationalists—those appreciating the efforts of traditionalists/denominationalists and seeking to learn from these efforts, yet striving to work together to move beyond the status quo toward fulfilling Christ's prayer for his people to be united, pure, and at peace with one another. Regretfully, both the traditionalists/denominationalists and the non-denominationalists only prolong church division through endless squabbles and debates. It is these groups who continue to tirelessly attempt to wear out the other

Author's Note

through their perpetual smugness and arrogance by a competing one-upmanship regarding whose side is more legitimate than the other. Today, we typically find those such as the so-called "social media apologists" too often dishearteningly embarrassing us all by exacerbating division rather than seeking to find solutions. Certainly, God's people deserve better.

It has often been said that effective communication requires a clear understanding of one's audience. In this case, my primary audience consists of two groups: *the shepherds of the church* and *the sheep of the church*. However, my main focus and loudest voice will be directed toward the shepherds.

Throughout history, it has been the leaders who have overwhelmingly led the sheep astray, not the other way around. Shepherds bear the responsibility for equipping the saints to stand firm against the enemy's attacks (Eph 4:12; 2 Tim 3:16–17), yet many have failed in this critical task. As a result, the average Christian today often lacks even the most basic tools for spiritual battle—both offensive and defensive (Eph 6:10–18).

Many believers struggle to hold confidence in absolute truth, leading to a fragile faith. They often have a poor grasp of the gospel, resulting in little assurance of salvation and an incomplete understanding of righteousness. Knowledge of Scripture—the believer's primary offensive weapon—is frequently shallow, and even when acquired, believers often lack the interpretive skills necessary to properly understand and apply what they read.

When shepherds lead their flocks astray with false doctrine or misguided practices, the consequences are devastating. These saints are often left vulnerable to a hostile, deceitful world or burdened with religious expectations that ultimately serve the leaders more than the sheep. This betrayal of trust leaves many defenseless and disheartened, unable to stand firm in their faith.

To the sheep of the church, I urge you to grow in the Christian faith and recognize that placing excessive devotion on a particular tradition, denomination, or movement does nothing to further God's kingdom. Instead, rise above these divisions and invest in the unity, peace, and purity of the church. Fixating on institutional

Author's Note

loyalties perpetuates division, often turning these institutions into idols that replace Christ in daily life. While well-meaning, such attachments stem from humanity's carnal nature, seeking security in religion rather than in Christ alone.

You may face resistance from leaders invested in preserving the status quo rather than pursuing the bold changes necessary to heal the church. Nevertheless, respectfully encourage them to think beyond their current frameworks and join you in seeking a more unified and faithful future. Ultimately, it may fall to the sheep to guide their shepherds.

It's important to emphasize that the Christian faith begins at home, not in the organized church. Families bear the primary responsibility for raising future generations of believers. Parents, grandparents, and all relatives must embrace this role, as God has entrusted them—not institutions—with the future of the faith.

For those who may not desire to read this manifesto in full, here is its essence: The root cause of division in the church originates in the "garden problem"—the conflict between two opposing worldviews born from creation and the fall: *theism* versus *humanism*. Humanism manifests as either philosophical or religious. Today's depiction of Christianity often falls into one of two categories: the *Christian faith* or the *Christian religion*. Understanding this foundational dichotomy clarifies the line between Christian theists and Christian humanists.

The challenge for the church is to purge herself of religion and reclaim the pure faith, grounded in theism. This reclamation is the only path to true unity, peace, and purity in Christ's bride. Humanism, with its man-made Christianized religion, sacrifices one or more of these essential elements. Only by adhering to God's revelation through theism in the reclamation of the Christian faith can the church hope to achieve reconciliation. As the apostle Paul writes,

> Therefore, if anyone is in Christ, he is a new creation. The old has passed away; behold, the new has come. All of this is from God, who through Christ reconciled us to himself and gave us the ministry of reconciliation; that is,

Author's Note

in Christ God was reconciling the world to himself, not counting their trespasses against them and entrusting to us the message of reconciliation. Therefore, we are ambassadors for Christ, God making his appeal through us. We implore you on behalf of Christ, be reconciled to God. (2 Cor 5:17–20)

Although this passage speaks primarily of reconciliation between God and humanity, it also applies to humanity within Christ's church. Reclaiming the faith and reconciling the church is essential for reflecting God's truth and glory in the world.

While it is true that positionally we as Christians have been reconciled to God through Christ, this does not mean that at times we cannot offend God or dishonor him in our lives and become estranged from him, thus requiring confession, repentance, and reconciliation. Similarly, it is also true that people can become estranged from one another, also requiring confession, repentance, and reconciliation. Throughout this manifesto, it will be reiterated that the church, by embracing religion and philosophy in varying forms and to varying degrees, has become increasingly poisoned by humanism and in great need of cleansing. As Christ purifies his church from these toxins, not only can reconciliation take place between Christ and his bride, but we as his bride can become reconciled one to another and better attain the peace and unity that he desires for his church. Far too long have too many of us spent too much time and energy protecting and promoting our particular tradition, denomination, or movement. It is long past time for Christians to grow up in the faith and begin to spend increasing time and energy in seeking to unify Christ's church as he longs to see us do. How can we think that we can stand before our Lord on that fateful day if all that we can do is explain and defend to him how we spent all our days promoting our particular group rather than striving to unify his people in all purity and peace as a witness before a lost and dying world. We must do this if we are to ever expect anyone to gain an interest in the gospel. We have no one to blame for failing to do so but ourselves.

Author's Note

As we approach these latter days, there are signs that Christ is actively moving to purify his bride, breaking down the walls of division that traditions, denominations, and movements have erected. This is cause for celebration! Yet, it also presents a profound challenge for those who have placed their identity and security in these constructs. For many, this will lead to a crisis of faith as they grapple with the realization that no single tradition is the "true church" or the "fullness" of Christianity.

This transformation will require patience and gentleness (Eph 4:1–7). It will be a monumental adjustment for those deeply entrenched in institutionalized religion to release the bonds of human constructs and embrace the freedom and light of the gospel. Such a shift will not happen overnight; it will be difficult and unsettling for many.

In a world growing increasingly humanistic, dark and challenging days lie ahead. Yet, as we anticipate the coming of the new Jerusalem, we can rest assured that our King and his church will prevail. This is not the time to lose heart. Instead, let us hold fast to the great hope set before us, trusting in the Lord's power to purify, unify, and glorify his church for his purposes and eternal kingdom.

> May the God of hope fill you with all joy and peace in believing, so that by the power of the Holy Spirit you may abound in hope. (Rom 15:13)

Prologue

SINCE ÉTIENNE COULD FIRST remember squinting his eyes to behold the stained-glass windows of his childhood church sanctuary, he had longed to see Christians united in one Lord, one faith, and one baptism (Eph 4:5). Growing up among culturally religious folks, he often wondered what God must think of a group of people who called themselves "Christians" or "Christ-followers," yet seemed to find little in common beyond Christ himself. Worse still, even Christ was sometimes misconstrued.

All around him, Étienne saw people representing various groups, denominations, and traditions—each somehow finding a reason to blame the others for the disunity or the scandal of a divided church. Often, these groups proclaimed themselves as the "true church" or the "fullness" of the body of Christ. Each had its own apologetic formulations to defend its position, clinging tightly to what were no doubt well-intended but flawed human constructs. As a child, Étienne sat puzzled: *What in the world happened all those years ago? Could the apostles have been so confused as to leave us with this mess? No wonder anyone in their right mind would hesitate to become a Christian.*

Indeed, who could seriously consider Christianity if they first understood how fractured and flawed its adherents have been? Despite long-standing traditions, colorful vestments, and splendid dwellings, the church seemed a divided house. Adding to the disillusionment were those who prided themselves on remaining "pure" from such divisions, often pointing fingers in self-righteousness while blind to their own religious inventions. At Pentecost, the church was one—no traditions, no denominations, no movements. And in the new Jerusalem, it will be the same: there will only be Christians. *How, then, did we get so sidetracked? How did we end up where we are today?*

And yet, Étienne knew he could not only accuse others. He had to confront his own shortcomings. Along with all the saints, he too had at times misunderstood and misrepresented the Christian faith. All have fallen short of the glory of God (Rom 3:23). There are none righteous—not even one (Rom 3:10). All stand guilty of following distorted notions of Christ, his church, and the precious faith in which they are called to partake. With this realization comes the desperate need for confession, repentance, and the humbling awareness of humanity's frailty before God's truth.

So how can the church attain unity without demanding uniformity, allowing for differences in culture, space, and time? How can the church pursue peace without compromising truth? And finally, how can the church seek purity while continually needing grace? These questions remain, as does the hope of God's marvelous grace to help us rise above our many shortcomings. Thus, the prayer must continue for the unity, peace, and purity of his church, that it may reflect his glory in this broken world.

While most theologians agree on the dates and events of Christian history, few seem able to explain why Christianity has developed as it has over two millennia. What shaped the thinking of the early church fathers, and what environmental influences led to their conclusions? Was their thinking always accurate, or were they, like us today, susceptible to the pressures and influences of their time? What presuppositions gave rise to the concept of "sacred" tradition? After all, did not Christ himself question—and at times condemn—the religious traditions of the Jewish clerical authorities of his day? Why, then, should the religious traditions of Christian clerics be considered any more valid?

Prologue

Could the church's continual struggle to claim legitimacy against competing ideas and heresies in its early centuries have led to the development of a hierarchical and authoritarian system, whether in Rome or Constantinople? What does it truly mean to be "catholic," "apostolic," or "orthodox"? And what of Protestantism—protesting what, and why? In their protests, could Protestants have unwittingly "thrown the baby out with the bathwater," reacting against what they saw as the evils of a Roman religious empire? Is there a difference between the "Christian religion" and the "Christian faith"? What, after all, was originally meant by "the Way" (Acts 9:2; 19:9)?

It is one thing for Christian communities to celebrate cultural distinctiveness, but quite another when such distinctiveness becomes doctrinal division. Over the centuries, the church has witnessed movements that have swung God's people from one extreme to another, searching desperately for new experiences, insights, or ways of living. At times, believers have found themselves spiritually empty, going through the motions or following a set liturgy each Sunday.

It is not surprising that God's people would yearn for something more real and meaningful. Scripture itself promises a genuine and intimate relationship with God, where believers can cry out, "Abba, Father" (Gal 4:6). This yearning has driven many to seek heroes of the faith, leading to the rise of Christian gurus with devoted followers. Revivals, pilgrimages, and retreats have sought to provide encounters with God. Others have pursued mysticism, social action, or even mass gatherings filled with fervor, "jamming for Jesus." Still others have sought solace in intellectual pursuits—devouring books, sermons, seminars, and conferences—or by returning to old traditions, crossing the Tiber or the Bosporus in search of spiritual security.

Amid this vast landscape, a central question remains: Is it possible to preserve cultural distinctiveness in expression without sacrificing doctrinal truth? Thankfully, we can trust that Christ has a plan for his church, even amid its brokenness.

Prologue

The following brief manifesto attempts to address some of these enduring questions. It does not presume to be the first or final word on the complexities of Christian history, nor does it claim to resolve the mire of division that characterizes modern Christianity. It is not aimed at the academic elite, who may dismiss its conclusions as naïve, simplistic, or fanciful (see appendix A). Rather, it is written in plain language for ordinary believers, offering straightforward reflections and practical hope.

The goal is to inspire believers in Christ to see a way forward in bringing healing to a fractured church. The prayer is particularly for those who tenaciously cling to their denominations or traditions, that they may grow in maturity and move beyond these divisions for the sake of Christ and his church. A watching world deserves to see the light of the gospel and understand why Jesus came into the world. Ultimately, it is not about us. It is about him.

SECTION 1

Where Did It All Begin?

WHEN THE TOPIC OF history arises, many respond dismissively, claiming that the "past is past" and cannot be changed. However, God views history differently. Throughout Scripture, the simple yet profound command to remember recurs repeatedly. It is often the failure—or refusal—to remember that leads to tragedy among God's people.

The present moment is fleeting, a nanosecond between the past and the future. Who we are today is profoundly shaped by our past, and it lays the foundation for who we will become. Without understanding the past, we cannot make wise decisions for the future. While knowledge is essential for decision-making, wisdom and discernment are even more crucial, for they guide knowledge toward truth and understanding.

In our modern world, we face an overload of information—a deluge of facts and data that often lacks the discernment needed to process it effectively. Without wisdom, this accumulation of knowledge becomes not only overwhelming but potentially dangerous. Our youth-oriented culture frequently equates maturity with acquiring knowledge and embracing the new, while

A Call to Unity, Peace, and Purity

disregarding the past as irrelevant. Yet true maturity comes from embracing the past, learning from it, and allowing it to shape us into wise and discerning individuals. Ignoring or running from the past is an act of cowardice that inevitably leads to disaster. Wisdom and discernment take time to develop and require the perspective that only age and reflection can provide. A society that elevates youthful exuberance at the expense of seasoned wisdom endangers its own future.

So, how does this emphasis on wisdom and discernment relate to the church's future? Quite profoundly, for understanding the church's past is essential for charting a way forward. Without such understanding, we risk perpetuating division and error.

From the very beginning, Satan has sought to divide God's people. His first act of deception in Eden was predicated on separation—tempting Eve apart from Adam. What was Adam doing during that fateful conversation? Where was he? Scripture does not provide specifics, but it is evident that some form of separation allowed Satan to deceive Eve. Even though Adam was with her when she ate the fruit (Gen 3:6), the initial opportunity for deception arose from division. This principle continues today: separation creates fertile ground for deception, both within the family and within the family of God.

The church is no exception. While theologians generally agree that the Christian church began at Pentecost (Acts 2:1–13), the people of God—the *ecclesia* or called-out ones—have existed since Adam. As Augustine observed, "The new is in the old concealed; the old is in the new revealed."[1] The church under the new covenant fulfills the promises of the old, forming an unbroken thread from Eden to the present day.

Yet humanity's fallen nature has a persistent tendency to try to improve upon God's design, often with noble but misguided intentions. Isaiah warned against this human inclination to substitute our thoughts for God's (Isa 55:8–9). Jesus himself condemned

---

1. See Augustine, *On the Spirit*, chapters 18 and 27 for this concept. Augustine did not use these exact words, but his thought has often been summarized with this phrase.

Where Did It All Begin?

the religious traditions of his day, which had distorted true faith into an institutionalized religion (Matt 15:1-9; Mark 7:1-13). Today, we risk making the same mistake, equating God's church with institutionalized Christianity. The church as an organized body is essential, but when it becomes a powerful Institution with a capital *I*, it risks losing sight of its true mission. The church is fundamentally about people; the faithful people of God going as far back in time as Adam and forward to Christ and his apostles and even to the poor, isolated widow ten years from now in a quiet corner of the world where no organized church has ever existed. Yet, this widow, because she has placed her trust in Christ, like so many others, is also part of the fullness of the body of Christ.

So, simply put, *the Christian faith is reality, as grasped from God's revelation, grounded in a relationship with him through Christ. Instead of being merely a religion, Christianity is "the Way"—God's designed path for human existence. It is the blueprint for living all of life!*

Jesus focused his condemnation not on pagan Rome but on the religious leaders who led God's people astray. Likewise, the church today must guard against internal corruption and division, for Satan's primary target has always been God's people. From the earliest days of the church, false teachings and heresies threatened its unity: gnostics, Judaizers, Ebionites, and others. Later centuries brought challenges from Arians, Montanists, Marcionites, and Donatists. The church's efforts to clarify doctrine and maintain catholicity through councils—beginning with Nicaea (325 CE)—often coincided with internal strife. Schisms followed: the Nestorian schism (431 CE), the Oriental Orthodox split (451 CE), the Great Schism (1054 CE), and the Protestant Reformation (1517 CE), leading to further fragmentation and denominationalism.

If God's will for his people is to dwell in unity, where do divisions come from? Scripture attributes them to human actions, often influenced by Satan (Rom 16:17-20; 1 Cor 1:10; Gal 5:20; Jude 19). A house divided cannot stand (Luke 11:17-20), and the church must remain vigilant against the forces that sow discord.

A Call to Unity, Peace, and Purity

Understanding the church's past is essential for addressing its present challenges and ensuring its future faithfulness. Only through the wisdom and discernment gained from history can we hope to chart a course that reflects Christ's will for his church: a unified, faithful, and living witness to the gospel.

Can the Church Ever Hope to Be "One"?

Throughout the Christian pilgrimage, so many of us think upon Jesus's high priestly prayer:

> that they may all be one, just as you, Father, are in me, and I in you, that they also may be in us, so that the world may believe that you have sent me. The glory that you have given me I have given to them, that they may be one even as we are one. (John 17:21–22)

We hold that the church is the "fullness" of Christ's body as being all members of his body:

> And he put all things under his feet and gave him as head over all things to the church, which is his body, the fullness of him who fills all in all. (Eph 1:22–23)

We take seriously the admonitions against division:

> I appeal to you, brothers, to watch out for those who cause divisions and create obstacles contrary to the doctrine that you have been taught; avoid them. (Rom 16:17)

> I appeal to you, brothers, by the name of our Lord Jesus Christ, that all of you agree, and that there be no divisions among you, but that you be united in the same mind and the same judgment. (1 Cor 1:10)

> Now the works of the flesh are evident: sexual immorality, impurity, sensuality, idolatry, sorcery, enmity, strife, jealousy, fits of anger, rivalries, dissensions, divisions, envy, drunkenness, orgies, and things like these. (Gal 5:19–20)

> "In the last time there will be scoffers, following their own ungodly passions." It is these who cause divisions, worldly people, devoid of the Spirit. (Jude 18–19)

Where Did It All Begin?

And, yet there continue to be those who adamantly hold their particular group, denomination, tradition, or movement as being exclusively the true church. Not only are such factions deceived in their conclusions, but these factions only foster a false sense of identity and security as well as arrogance and pride among their members. Finally, these factions only perpetuate discord and division in the church.

The First Ecumenical Council of Constantinople (381 CE) asserts, "We believe in one holy catholic and apostolic Church" as the four marks of the church.[2]

- One—expressing unity
- Holy—being set apart
- Catholic—being universal
- Apostolic—holding to the teachings of the apostles as derived from the Holy Scriptures

However, tragically, such aforesaid factions continually try to reinterpret the above four marks in such a way as to support and legitimize their faction as being the "one true church."

In the recent past, there have been several ecumenical attempts to bring the church to unity, all leading to failure. The problem is that these noble, yet misguided, attempts have not succeeded because of the inability to grasp the fundamental problem as to why the church has become fractured in the first place. This problem is a worldview problem, which will be addressed later in our discussion.

One of these failed attempts has been *unilateralism*, which is the idea that "we want to be united but ultimately only under our church tradition, denomination, movement, group, etc." Really? Does anyone seriously believe that this could ever happen? Simply believing that everyone else will just give up and surrender their deeply held theological positions that have been fought over for hundreds of years, at times even to the point of bloodshed? Those who would even think this is a reasonable option would either be

---

2. Nicene Creed.

blind out of their arrogance or have little true understanding of the real issues at stake. This will simply never happen.

A second failed attempt has been in some sort of *pan/transdenominationalism*, holding some sort of "United Nations" approach. This approach seems to say, "orthodoxy really does not matter so much, only that we are inclusive and united." This is the position representing groups such as the World Council of Churches. Again, noble, and well-intended, but false in that truth is seen as merely a human construction rather than stemming from God's revelation. As a result, there remains very little in absolute terms of what encompasses the Christian faith, leaving just a bunch of good people trying to do good things in the hope of making the world a better place.

Experientialism may be described as trying to unite the church based on shared spiritual experiences. For example, many Christians recall the 1960s and 1970s of the charismatic movement, ever hopeful that if all Christians could experience the "second blessing" of the baptism of the Holy Spirit, this shared experience would be the one thing that would overcome all differences and unite us in the Christian faith. While shared experiences can be quite warming to our hearts, there is still the issue of truth that is propositional and can never be left to experience alone. Thus, just placing our hope in commonly shared experiences will not be enough to bring us together when reality must confront propositional truth that must be addressed outside of one's experience.

And finally, what most Christians encounter today is what may be described as *fatalistic pacifism*, the belief that nothing ultimately matters except that we do not fight among ourselves and that we must merely love and accept one another. Just claiming to know Jesus is enough, even if "Jesus" is defined as whoever or whatever we want him to be. Tolerance is the reigning religious notion, where intolerance is not to be tolerated. Love is all we need since, ultimately, Jesus is love. Again, truth is something to be negotiated. Never mind who Jesus actually is and why he himself proclaimed he came into the world. In answering Pilate, Jesus said, "'For this purpose I was born and for this purpose I have come into the world—to bear witness to the truth. Everyone who is of the truth listens to my voice.' Pilate said to him, 'What is truth?'" (John 18:37–38). Ah yes, that continual problem of "truth." Jesus facing death was not the kind of king who was ready to negotiate on this crucial matter.

In what might be seen as a very positive development, there have been several recent attempts at reconciliation stemming from a major shift in thinking by the Roman Catholic Church in the mid-1960s resulting from Vatican II. Examples are found in the Balamand Statement with the Orthodox Church (1993); Evangelicals and Catholics Together (1994); the *Joint Declaration on the Doctrine of Justification* with the Lutheran World Federation (1999); Christian Churches Together in the USA (2001); the Joint International Commission for Theological Dialogue Between the Catholic Church and the Oriental Orthodox Churches (2003); and the *Declaration on the Way* with the Evangelical Lutheran Church in America (2016). However, until the foundational issue of authority is agreed on, regretfully, such steps are only token measures, and the church will forever remain divided. Until we reach a common understanding of where authoritative truth is derived, that of a truly Christian theistic worldview, unity is not possible.

A Way Forward While Learning from Our Past

What is being proposed here is neither a new tradition nor denomination nor movement—but rather a better understanding or perspective—a way of seeing beyond our more traditional stereotypical notions. We need a faith that is orthodox, yet beyond "Eastern"; evangelical, yet beyond "Protestant"; and catholic, yet beyond "Roman." The attempt is to bring greater clarity to what we all hope to call, the "apostolic" faith of the church. This faith is (1) orthodox, espousing that the Scriptures are held to be the only infallible rule of faith and practice by which all things are evaluated and upholding the essential doctrines of what may be called Christian—an understanding that comes out of a truly Christian theistic worldview. This faith is also (2) evangelical (*euangelion*,

Gk., or *evangelium*, Lat.) espousing that the gospel—good news—is found in the reconciliation of God and humanity through Christ (his life, death, burial, resurrection, and ascension). This reconciliation is made possible only by God's grace through faith in Christ's final work. Thus, the focus of Christ's church is on him alone. Being evangelical is being Christocentric. And finally, this faith is (3) catholic, espousing that Christ's church is universal throughout the earth. The church is the "fullness of him who fills all in all" (Eph 1:22-23). The church is composed of all who are in him (John 3:3-7; 1 Pet 1:3-5, 22-23). In the apostle Paul's letter to the Romans, he clearly summarizes that those who are in Christ are saved through confessing that Jesus is Lord and in believing that God raised him from the dead (Rom 10:9). This sounds rather definitive.

Sometimes, when asked if a particular tradition, denomination, or movement is truly Christian, a wise response has often been to contrast "content" between a particular "container" or "label" on the container. For example, content can be placed in various containers having numerous labels. The main issue is the content that is held within the container. At times containers may have problematic content or very little content at all. Labels can also be misleading. The Christian faith has a particular content. In the end, it is the content that matters. Our various man-made structures and labels will one day pass away, while it is the content that is eternal. One day, the labels of Roman Catholic, Greek Orthodox, or Baptist will be a matter of antiquity. However, the truth as espoused in the Christian faith will remain forever. We are reminded in Matt 23:25-26 of Jesus's rebuke of the scribes and Pharisees about their concern with utensils while missing the importance of the content. Similarly, the apostle Paul had to warn the church at Corinth about overly esteeming and venerating various Christian leaders and identifying with these leaders to the point of causing division in the church (1 Cor 1:10-17; 3:1-9). He goes on to remind the Corinthians that we as God's people are only temporal jars of clay (2 Cor 4:7) bearing a great treasure. It is this precious treasure that we are to focus our affections on and not upon particular people. Why some Christians insist on identifying themselves as Benedictines, Augustinians, Thomists, Lutherans, Wesleyans, Calvinists, or whoever is beyond comprehension if one is to take seriously the apostle's warnings. It is also quite doubtful as to whether many of these leaders would have ever in the slightest way welcomed their followers to mark themselves in identifying with their names. John Calvin, for example, detested the term "Calvinism."[1]

While the living out of the Christian faith may be expressed somewhat differently according to time and culture, the content of the Christian faith remains unchangeable in that it is based upon God's infallible revelation. The historical problem is that both the faith and Christ's church have been "packaged" poorly as some sort of religion derived out of a Greco-Roman-Medieval world; and for far too long, they have sorely needed to be "repackaged" as originally intended. We must regain the proper perspective in that the faith is not a religion but rather a way of life. The church is not primarily some formalized institution but rather the family of God. Furthermore, we must never lose sight of the fact that the Christian church is Christ's church, and it is he alone who calls those who are his to himself. It is Christ alone who saves. We must never elevate the bride above the bridegroom. While the bride and bridegroom retain a oneness in their relationship; they are not the same. The church is not Christ nor does she, out of her own being, emanate the authority of Christ. Such a notion would be blasphemy. Again, the shepherd and the sheep share a relationship, but each exists separately with very distinctive attributes. While the church may be called as a witness to proclaim the gospel whereby those who are his may be saved, the church cannot save anyone. Such a notion would make no sense whatsoever in that the church cannot save herself. The church only represents Christ by her witness; the church does not replace Christ. While we can and should love his church as he loves his church, we must never confuse the two.

Finally, we must ever be mindful that we are in a spiritual war with Satan (2 Cor 11:12–15; Eph 6:10–20; 1 Pet 5:8–11; 1

A Call to Unity, Peace, and Purity

John 2:18–27; 5:19). Satan always seeks to deceive God's people by appearing to be good and godly, yet he is extremely cunning in causing division and destruction, starting with our individual lives, then within relationships—particularly within families, then within the church and eventually within society at large. Satan consistently offers a counterfeit to the truth. Even from the garden onward, he is a liar and the father of lies (John 8:44) coming to us as an "angel of light" (2 Cor 11:14), often twisting the truth and ever offering a false truth by playing to our weaknesses, blinding us to God, to ourselves, and to the world around us. Without a doubt, if our eyes were truly opened and we were able to see the amount of demonic activity that has taken place both in the past as well as presently within Christianity, cold chills would permeate our beings, leaving us quite shocked and alarmed.

Although a common lament often heard concerns the lack of spiritual vitality in modern culture, one must attest that while there may be a lack of Christian spiritual fever, there is certainly no lack of spiritual interest. One must wonder why science fiction films such as the *Star Wars* saga by George Lucas keep audiences coming back again and again. While no doubt there are numerous reasons for the popularity of *Star Wars*, one cannot overlook the spiritual core of the altered "eastern mysticism" of "the Force" that permeates the storyline. While contemporary thinking may proclaim that the concepts of good and evil are merely human constructs, people still find themselves convinced that there must truly be some real notion of good and evil in the universe. People still find themselves praying that they too will not one day succumb to some form of an evil empire; and if this should ever come to pass, without hesitation they would hope that there would appear a promised savior to rescue them from certain doom.

The good news is there is much for which to be thankful and there is a real reason for such hope. As has been stated, Christ has established his true church with his instructions for governance and authority. The church exists regardless of the mess that we have made because the church is his church, and the gates of hell will not prevail because he is building his church and not us! We just need to bring ourselves in line with him. We must come to grips with the fact that while none of the expressions of the church that we have developed is exclusively his church, each of these expressions has, to varying degrees, attempted to reflect Christ's church. This understanding is the "ground zero" from which all future discussions can be entered into and upon which any hope of unity, peace, and purity can be found.

SECTION 2

The Age-Old Problem

The "Garden Problem"

IT MAY BE CALLED "life's ultimatum." What happened in the garden of Eden set the course of human history and particularly, the history of God's people. In Gen 3:1–7 the Scriptures state,

> Now the serpent was more crafty than any other beast of the field that the Lord God had made. He said to the woman, "Did God actually say, 'You shall not eat of any tree in the garden'?" And the woman said to the serpent, "We may eat of the fruit of the trees in the garden, but God said, "You shall not eat of the fruit of the tree that is in the midst of the garden, neither shall you touch it, lest you die." But the serpent said to the woman, "You will not surely die. For God knows that when you eat of it your eyes will be opened, and you will be like God, knowing good and evil." So when the woman saw that the tree was good for food, and that it was a delight to the eyes, and that the tree was to be desired to make one wise, she took of its fruit and ate, and she also gave some to her husband who was with her, and he ate. Then the eyes of both were opened, and they knew that they were naked. And they sewed fig leaves together and made themselves loincloths.

The Age-Old Problem

Here we find the basic formula of Satan's deception: either (1) to question the credibility of God's word or one's ability to comprehend God's word (*"Did God actually say?"*) or (2) to infer the inadequacy of God's word as not being fully complete or sufficient for one to live in obedience to God, and, thus, in need of amending or of further clarification (*suggesting to Eve that God had not given her the full story*). Nevertheless, the pivotal issue at stake was Eve's temptation to "be like God." Not the issue of being created in his image; that was settled. Not the issue of reflecting God's character or morality; that was plain. It was the issue of being "like God, knowing good and evil," that was the problem. It was desiring to be "like God" in his being, as Lord over all, with all wisdom, authority, and power in being able to "know" good and evil while remaining sovereign over all. It was seeking those attributes reserved for God alone: his omniscience, his omnipotence, his omnipresence. It was this essential problem that banished man from the garden (Gen 3:22–24). It was the problem of man claiming to be like God regarding his authority and setting our desires upon that which alone is exclusively his. Hmm . . . where have we seen this before? Recalling the classical theological understanding that Lucifer or Satan (the devil) was once an angel who rebelled, desiring to be "like God," and as a result being cast into perdition with all his allies (demons), we can see a similar scenario with humanity—God's greatest creation, the only aspect of creation that was created in his image. If Satan, condemned to destruction, could not defeat God himself, why not try to defeat as many of God's image-bearers as possible to join him in his eternal destiny?

Therefore, Eve, being innocent of sin at the time, was essentially tricked and deceived into thinking that being like God, to make herself all-wise, was a good thing. Can we not still see this continual deception in play throughout history? The lifelong battle is to either choose "God to be God" or in some sordid way to choose "us to be God," by creating a god or gods or essentially making ourselves to be God. Any time we set ourselves to be the final authority for what is true or right, we fall into this same abyss. So, where did Satan focus his attack? His focus was, and continues to be today, to attack the truth by twisting and deceiving ("Did God *actually* say?"). Bit by bit, moment by moment, Satan slithers his way into the church, God's people, somehow convincing them, either individually or corporately, that God's truth is simply not enough—there *must* be something more man can do or offer. Furthermore, Satan's deception is a warning to all, that anytime individuals or groups of individuals claim to speak with the infallible authority of God regarding any doctrine unsupported by God's revelation as found in the Scriptures, or claim to be his infallible interpreters, such voices are literally "dancing with the devil" in falling prey to Lucifer's lust to have an authority reserved for God alone.

Throughout the ages, there has continually been a debate over the nature of man and creation. The basic question is: Is man/creation naturally good or evil? One might say that man/creation being created and proclaimed by God as "good" would naturally mean that man/creation in today's world would naturally be good. Others might say that man/creation is now fallen, and thus is under the curse of God and is now evil. Often people have difficulty holding to the dignity of man/creation while concurrently holding to the supremacy of God. In the final analysis, most orthodox theologians would attest that even though creation is under the curse, resulting in an unnatural "groaning" (Rom 8:22), there is still the "blueprint" of his original good design that can be comprehended and experienced (Rom 1:20).

While man is created in the image of God and as such will always have intrinsic worth and value, he is now cursed and therefore his nature is under this curse of death, both physically and spiritually. Man, in his unredeemed state, is described as "ungodly," even an "enemy" against God (Rom 5:6–11). Only through redemption found in Christ alone can man find hope in his being declared righteous and in being sanctified and transformed (John 17:17; Rom 12:2; Eph 5:5; 1 Thess 5:23).

The Age-Old Problem
Revelation, Philosophy and Religion

Revelation may be defined as "an act of revealing or communicating divine truth" or as "something that is revealed by God to humans."[2] Basically, revelation emanates from God, not man. Because special or divine revelation as given to God's people ended with Christ and with apostolic teaching (Acts 2:42; Eph 2:20; Jude 3), the notion of continued revelation outside of the Scriptures that would be promoted as universal doctrine for God's people would fall under human tradition or religion. Because of this temptation, there are numerous warnings not to add to what God says (Deut 4:2, 12:32; Prov 30:6; 1 Cor 4:6; Rev 22:18). General or natural revelation found in creation is also an important part of revelation. However, because of the fallenness of the natural world, this "natural" revelation can only rightfully be discerned as it is consistent with divine revelation (which is not under the curse). Therefore, while natural revelation can point toward the existence of God, God cannot be rightfully known outside of divine revelation. Therefore, the Logos (Word), found in the divine revelation of Christ and in the Scriptures, is necessary for one to rightfully grasp God's revelation in this world. Doctrine can never be primarily based upon natural revelation or natural law in that divine revelation is necessary in a fallen world to confirm what is truly natural and what is not.

Philosophy may be defined as "a particular system of beliefs, values, and principles"; "the study of the nature of reality and existence, of what it is possible to know, and of right and wrong behavior."[3] Basically, philosophy is humanity's "natural" understanding of the world. The apostle Paul, well-acquainted with the various philosophies of his day in the Greco-Roman world, warned the church at Colossae not to be taken "captive" by philosophy (Col 2:8) describing such as empty deceit according to the elemental spirits of the world and not according to Christ. And yet, there is something even more cunning than philosophy—religion.

Religion may be defined as "a cause, principle, or system of beliefs held to with ardor and faith."[4] Furthermore, religion may be described as "human beings' relation to that which they regard as holy, sacred, absolute, spiritual, divine, or worthy of especial reverence."[5] In many ways, religion is not unlike philosophy, except that its focus may be on that which is spiritual or supernatural. Like philosophy, religion, in principle, is derived from humanity, not from God. A vital fact that cannot be overstated is that Christ did not come into the world to establish some new religion—there were plenty of religions already present. The essence of the Christian faith is that of revelation, not religion. In the New Testament, the word "religion/religious" (*threeskia/threeskos*, Gk.) is mentioned in only a handful of passages—mostly relating to religions or religious activity derived from surrounding religions. The apostle Paul particularly describes Judaism as a "religion" in Acts 25:19 and Acts 6:5 and in a more general sense in Col 2:23. In the apostle James' letter (Jas 1:26–27), "religion" or being "religious" refers to those who were bragging about their great devotion or spirituality, regardless of works. James corrects this sense of religiosity (devotion) as being false and in that a true sense of religion (devotion) includes works. James is not implying that the Christian faith is in any way a religion in the sense of a human-derived system; rather, it is God-derived. Sadly, one of the greatest tragedies of Christian history (which has led to a false understanding of the Christian faith as well as that of the church) occurred when the Christian faith came to be understood and proclaimed as a religion, resulting in the Christian faith being relegated to being merely a religion among other religions. It cannot be emphasized enough how destructive such a notion has been in corrupting the testimony of Christ and his church.

While it can certainly be attested that in almost all Christian traditions and denominations the term "religion" has commonly been fully embraced in describing many aspects of Christianity, in recent years there has been a growing concern about seeing religion as Satan's counterfeit for the true Christian faith and in seeking how to rid the church of the notion of Christianity as a religion. Much of this interest initially occurred as twentieth-century Swiss theologian Karl Barth (1886–1968) provocatively suggested, in his

The Age-Old Problem

theological magnum opus, *Church Dogmatics*, that "the revelation of God [is] the sublimation [abolition] of religion."[6] While many Christian theologians did not particularly endorse all of Barth's theological understandings, this comment did generate some interest regarding the place of "religion" in Christian discussion.

In the late 1960s, a quaint little book became very popular among Christians. It was entitled *How to Be a Christian Without Being Religious* (1967), by Fritz Ridenour. Basically, in his book, the author, using the letter of the apostle Paul to the Romans as a template, examined the validity of religion within the Christian life. Since Ridenour was relatively unknown at that time and was neither considered a respected academic nor theologian, many theologians and church leaders dismissed the book as mere rubbish only to be appreciated by an uneducated lay audience. However, the book went on to sell over 1.5 million copies as the commoner in the pews began to question whether the established institutional church had increasingly evolved to become a bastion of man-made religion, where people simply went through the motions or entertained themselves with religious games. If this was indeed the case, then maybe the everyday Christian was being "played" by an elite clergy class desperately holding on to their job security by threatening the parishioner with some form of damnation for not going along with the status quo. While the book was not originally intended to be an attack upon the church but rather written to challenge the individual Christian in living out a more genuine life in Christ, the established church nevertheless became a target for scrutiny. After all, this was the revolutionary 1960s, where "the establishment" in *any* form was counted as an object of suspicion.

Today, as the understanding of the concept of worldview has entered common discourse, it is increasingly argued that both religion and philosophy are, in essence, a product of a humanistic worldview of life in that both stem from humanity, as opposed to revelation, which flows from God, a theistic worldview. This understanding, in a nutshell, reflects the "garden problem": man vs. God. Plainly, the crucial issue that the church faces is the challenge of trying to discern the *Christian faith* as distinct from the *Christian religion*. Furthermore, even though the last two thousand years have experienced rapid growth in the expansion of the Christian faith, serious questions remain as to the depth and orthodoxy in understanding, as well as in the practice of, what it means to be Christian.

The Harmful Nature of Religion

As previously stated, it is religion that Satan most often uses to deceive us because it embraces the spiritual dimension of our thinking. As Satan's counterfeit, religion is humanity's idea of the spiritual world as opposed to God's idea of the spiritual world found in his revelation. Religion often embraces a *cultus* (Lat.), comprising established or accepted religious rites or customs of worship. It is also from *cultus* that such words as "cult," "cultivate," and "culture" are derived. All these words consist of the same underlying notion of something that stems from or develops out of the influence of humanity. As long as one recognizes the origin of *cultus* as that which comes from humanity rather than from God, then discretion can be used in how the Christian faith interacts with notions of cult, cultivation, or culture. For example, we all live within a particular culture that encompasses an existence within a certain place and time. Because of this, the Christian faith (being supra-cultural and timeless) must always be lived out within a particular culture. This is not a problem if culture is held in distinction to the content of which the faith consists. However, when culture is allowed to determine the content of the faith, then the faith falls prey to the danger of being corrupted by the ideas of humanity. For example, while culture may influence a particular pattern of worship by God's people at a certain time and place in history, a particular cultural application of worship does not warrant what is to be held as the only true expression of acceptable worship for God's people for all time.

Inevitably, one will argue that New Testament Christianity is simply an extension of Old Testament Judaism. Therefore, since

The Age-Old Problem

Judaism is certainly filled with a great deal of religion, this would justify religion continuing in Christianity. While volumes can be written on the relationship between the faith of God's people before the advent of Christ and afterwards, one must always be reminded that Christ came to fulfill, to finalize, all that was foreshadowed in incomplete ways in the life and faith of God's people as expressed before Christ. While God laid out very rudimentary expressions of worship and life in concrete forms in the old covenant, even utilizing notions that would appear to be religious (e.g., sacrifices, priests, rituals/ceremonial laws, etc.), these were only to be held as primitive and temporary forms representing eternal truths to be actualized ultimately in Christ. A similar comparison might be made if one thinks about the way children are educated in comparison to how adults are educated. With children, often more concrete forms are utilized because children cannot think and process ideas in abstract forms. Only as children mature toward adulthood can ideas be grasped and reasoned abstractly. Even more so, in the Old Testament, early forms were intended not as some separate religious expression in the life of God's people, but as expressions intrinsic to normative life. Yet, not unlike the church of today, God's people under the old covenant, not being satisfied with God's revelatory instructions, went on to add their own religious ideas, resulting in what became Judaism, the Jewish religion in the time of Christ. We are reminded that it was precisely these humanistic religious ideas that were the most offensive to Jesus.

Religion, being Satan's counterfeit, is derived essentially from a lie, from that which is false, leading to deception. Religion appears as "an angel of light," which may be seductive and beckons us away from the truth. One can easily become captivated by religion and brought into bondage. Sadly, to the degree that a particular expression of Christianity embraces religion, those who adhere to that expression expose themselves to the danger of deception. The result is that such a person can become deceived and can find themselves in bondage to elements of that expression. This is most clearly seen when Christians place their focus more on a particular expression of Christianity rather than on Christ himself. When being Protestant, Orthodox, or Catholic takes center stage rather than Christ, trouble follows.

Often, in religion, that which might originally be seen as merely customary can evolve into that which may become obligatory. Practices or observances, once merely a voluntary expression of culture, may through time slowly become incorporated into a norm of religious life to be expected by a religious body. Failing to follow such norms may be seen as not being faithful or religious. Examples of such norms might be in the observance of certain religious days or the veneration of particular holy persons, or saints. Believers can easily be seduced into believing that if such norms are not kept, somehow their standing before God might become jeopardized. The potential for inflicting a false sense of guilt for not keeping such norms is quite high.

Finally, there is the danger of religion becoming addictive. Some may even compare religious addiction as similar in effect to an addiction to pornography: a type of "spiritual pornography." Unlike philosophy, which tends to be more cerebral, religion may often include powerful elements such as passion and emotion. Being spiritual in nature, religion can reach down into the deepest levels of a person's soul. Similarly, while a person's sexuality is a legitimate and wonderful part of the human constitution enjoyed with another in the intimate bonds of marriage, pornography corrupts this God-given gift with deception, a false notion of what true sexuality represents. In like manner, religion corrupts the soul by presenting a deception of the truth found in God's revelation. Certainly, declaring that religion is akin to "spiritual porn" no doubt sounds rather harsh to our more timid, traditional ears. However, as one comes to recognize how damaging the counterfeit of pornography is on true sexuality, it becomes a bit nauseating as one is awakened to the realization of how religion has altered true spirituality. Again, religion is a counterfeit, a cheap knockoff, of true spirituality. Sadly, as the deception of religion grows, it increasingly becomes addictive and may consume a person. Often, such addiction is further enhanced through spiritual

The Age-Old Problem

activities such as religious rituals, repetitive prayer and/or bodily movements, chanting, altered states of consciousness, and other methods of imprinting religion into a person's psyche. Breaking religious addiction can be extremely difficult. Strangely enough, in this context, religion can certainly be the "opium of the people."[7] However, God's revelation and true faith in Christ is the solution and the antidote to religious addiction.

While the early church fathers during the first half-millennium of church history can be thanked for helping to summarize and define some essential truths of the Christian faith and for striving to maintain unity in the church, sadly, they can also be blamed for introducing a great deal of religious humanism into the theology and practice of the church. Regretfully, religious humanism increasingly became mainstream and cemented into the thinking of the medieval church, only to become challenged during the Reformation. Somehow the church slowly lost her original identity as essentially being a "called out community" of God's people who live together as a family, a chosen people group of the Christian faith, rather than as a highly organized and structured religious institution. Again, while some degree of form is always necessary in all of life, it is important that form not rob life of its vitality.

Worldview

In recent years, the concept of worldview (German: *Weltanschauung*) has become a rather popular topic for conversation. Essentially, a worldview is how we see the world. The concept of worldview was first introduced by Immanuel Kant in 1790 and was later more fully expounded on by German thinkers such as Hegel, Humboldt, Heidegger, and Jaspers during the 1800–1900s. By the late 1800s and early 1900s reformed Christian theologians, James Orr (Scotland) and Abraham Kuyper (The Netherlands) began to see the significance of this perspective. Later the concept became popularized in the mid- and later 1900s by evangelical thinkers such as Francis Schaeffer and James W. Sire. This important breakthrough in philosophical and theological understanding led to a far more comprehensive grasp of the history and development of human thought, especially in answering the question "From where do ideas originate?" While earlier Christian thinkers such as Augustine, Aquinas, Luther, and Calvin certainly left much for the church to ponder, these earlier thinkers could only speak out of the cultural understanding and language of the times in which they lived. The concept of worldview had not yet entered the philosophical landscape.

In contemporary discussion, this concept has often been broken down into numerous worldviews. However, this manifesto concludes that these many worldview expressions are better described as merely "paradigms" and can essentially be boiled down to the garden problem. By saying this, I am suggesting that only two valid worldviews exist when discussing truth: humanism and theism. While one may claim to be a nihilist (i.e., holding that life is meaningless in that no truth exists), it is quite difficult to find anyone who can consistently live as such. To live consistently as a nihilist, one must eventually take their own life (and at times, others with them). In the end, one will either live as a theist (holding God as God) or as a humanist (holding man as God). Simply: we can choose to see the world from God's perspective (theism) or we can choose to see the world from a human perspective (humanism). There is nowhere else to go; hence, the garden problem. Time after time, it is quite assuring that over the course of history many of the ideas that humanity may come up with as being "new" or "novel" may find root in God's infallible word. Too often the word of God is readily shortchanged or dismissed as being irrelevant.

In returning to the garden of Eden in Gen 3, we can see the essential dilemma facing humanity regarding how we see the world or universe: we can choose to see the world or universe either (1) through God's eyes (theism) or (2) through man's eyes (humanism). Theism focuses on God's revelation while humanism focuses on man's abilities. In a fallen world, man is imperfect, fallible, and unable to see clearly. Man can only see through a lens dimly (1 Cor 13:12). Therefore, man's vision is distorted, and he sees things incompletely or falsely, leading to a counterfeit interpretation of life.

The Age-Old Problem

Even his understanding of what is natural or unnatural is impaired and further compromised by the fact that the natural universe as originally created by God has also been distorted by the fall. As a result, if man turns from God's revelation (God's word) to find the answers, he must then rely upon his own abilities to develop explanations for what he experiences. These explanations are rooted in philosophy and religion. God never originally intended for man to live out of either one of these standpoints. Both stem from doubting God's word, either in (1) questioning the credibility of God's word or one's ability to comprehend it or (2) insinuating that God's word is not sufficient for one to live life as it was meant to be lived as pleasing to God. Again, this is not saying that there are other things that one may discover in life that may help us live life as we apply this knowledge. The implication is that God has not given humanity sufficient information in his word as to how to live a life pleasing to him.

One may then immediately exclaim that "theism" and "God" may mean many different things to many people. What about the concept of God according to Islam, Judaism, Hinduism, Buddhism, pantheism, deism, etc.? Certainly, this observation is quite important to any discussion of theism and most rightfully should be held. However, it is readily acknowledged that because of the particular focus at hand, which limits time and space, it will happily be conceded that what is meant by "theism" is precisely Christian theism. Furthermore, when "humanism" is discussed, it is not modern humanism rooted in the more recent scholarly traditions of the Renaissance or Enlightenment periods of history, whether secular or religious, that is being considered. "Humanism" as referenced here, is the more comprehensive worldview espousing that all things comprising truth are subject to man. This worldview stands in direct contrast to theism, which espouses that all things comprising truth are subject to God. The essential conflict of these opposing worldviews pits religion/philosophy as Satan's counterfeit against that of God's revelation. For example, a common misperception of humanists portrays theism as depicting God as being against humanity. However, this is not the case, as theism seeks to rightfully portray humanity as created in God's image and, as such, of immeasurable worth. Regretfully, as a result of the fall, under humanism, natural or carnal man now seeks to distort and exalt humanity. Theism seeks to restore man to a right relationship with God and a right relationship within himself. God is not at war with humanity; God is at war with humanism.

Some may counter with the fact that often philosophers or religionists may, at times, have described phenomena that would be noted as that which is also found in revelation. This, without question, is most certain. However, because unregenerate man cannot rightfully comprehend the thoughts of God, he is left to his own imagination in interpreting revelation because he does not have the Spirit of God (1 Cor 2:11–16). Regretfully, man's carnal nature does not understand the world correctly and his heart is darkened to the truth (Rom 1:16–25). While revelation found in the natural world might point to the fact that there is a God, it is only through divine revelation and by the Holy Spirit that a person can be brought into a relationship with God. In sum, humanism focuses on man and his abilities while theism focuses on God and his grace and glory.

In the end, we must come to understand that there are essentially only two worldviews that humanity can hold: humanism or theism. As has been stated, this stems from the garden problem. Humanism can take one of two forms: philosophical humanism (often referred to as "secularism") or religious humanism ("religion"). Both can claim to have the voice of infallible authority that can only be ascribed to God alone. Philosophical humanism denies the spiritual side of life whereas religion embraces spirituality. However, both seek to exalt humanity and human ability either directly or indirectly. Of the two, religion can become the more deceptive by those who embrace spirituality in that while proclaiming to focus on the spiritual nature of life, religion relies on man to define spiritual truth in contrast to theism, which relies solely on revelation to define spiritual truth. This is often done by those who would seek to add to or to take away from God's word as the sole authority on which Christian doctrine is to be established, holding that the Scriptures alone are not sufficient as the basis for living the Christian life. As previously stated, to combat this temptation, God has consistently warned his people against the tendency to go beyond the Scriptures (Deut 4:2; 12:32; Prov 30:6; Rev 22:18).

The primary problem throughout the history of God's people is where Satan has tempted and deceived the people of God into failing to see where humanism has "entered the camp" and captivated hearts and minds, whereby worldly religion and philosophy are syncretized with revelation, producing heterodoxy (a mixture of heresy and orthodoxy). It would seem as if that ancient serpent unceasingly deceives humanity with his forked tongue, hissing philosophy and religion into their vulnerable ears. Today, the church is being challenged to return to the firm foundation of Christ, built upon the precious stones of revelation rather than those of religion, which in the end will burn (1 Cor 3:10–15). In essence, we must recognize that the church is in the midst of a spiritual battle that continually rages from within. As to a worldview, this is "theism vs. humanism." Philosophically, this is "Christian theism vs. religious humanism." As to the church, this is "the Christian faith vs. the Christian religion." The future church must courageously engage in this internal spiritual warfare and rise to challenge Satan's attempts to lead God's people astray. Jesus reminds us of this battle, even in the "latter days," where even the elect are tempted to be led astray (Matt 24:22–24; Mark 13:20). We must pray that God's people will come to realize that they may have mistakenly placed their well-intended faith in the wrong things, such as church affiliation, sacraments, good works, or spiritual disciplines (even though all may have their rightful place), rather than in their reliance on Christ alone for their salvation. While there is certainly the battle with the outside pagan world to be encountered, it is the battle within the church that is even more pressing. A house divided against itself will not stand (Mark 3:22–27). Once Christianity began to portray itself as a religion, it unwittingly wedded itself to Lucifer's playbook. It is time for the people of God to stand up and resist Satan's counterfeit religion within the church. It is time to revisit Christ's initial warnings in the book of Revelation to remind us that behind the curtain, an intense spiritual battle is ever-present.

Throughout the centuries the deception of a Christianized religious humanism has too often captivated the hearts and minds of God's people, poisoning Christ's bride. The present call is to seek to clean up our own house and become brutally aware of what it is that much of the organized church has been selling her people. Although this call might appear as coming from some simple-minded alarmist, it may also be suggested that Christ may very well be warning his church. We must humbly realize that God never intended religion or philosophy to be that which would reference or describe himself or his relation to humanity. God's revelation of himself and his purposes is that of reality and encompasses the truth of how life is intended to be lived. Religion and philosophy flow from the mind of man, not from the mind of God. Tragically, it is the "professional religionists," the clergy and the theologians, who like those before them, such as the scribes and the Pharisees, cling most tightly to and perpetuate religion. Moreover, it is extremely upsetting to realize that so many of us have unwittingly indoctrinated others to become addicted and "hooked" on religion, resulting in their dependence upon and coming under bondage to our religious institutions. Sadly, one can become captivated by religion to such a degree as to become deceived regarding whom or what they are serving. Those who interpret the Scriptures must cease approaching God's word with a preconceived grid of religion rather than that of revelation. The Bible is not some religious writing but is a record of God's divine revelation to humanity. *As long as God's relationship to humanity is continually being understood and proclaimed as being that of religion rather than that of reality, that which would be called "Christianity" will be misconstrued as well as misrepresented and, therefore, will be doomed to quite a troubled future.*

In summation, it is upon the following premise that this manifesto is being set forth. This premise claims that in the beginning there was God. It was God who created the universe and humanity. Before the fall, humanity operated entirely within a theistic worldview, fully trusting in God. As a result of the fall, a competing, deceptive worldview, now understood as humanism, entered the arena of life, causing humanity to doubt God. Out of this humanistic worldview flowed philosophy and religion. Philosophy seeks to describe life from a non-spiritual standpoint, whereas religion seeks to describe life from a spiritual standpoint. Philosophy primarily seeks to question the credibility of God and/or his revealed word ("Did God actually say?") whereas religion, although possibly recognizing the legitimacy of God and his revealed word, questions God's full disclosure ("You will not surely die. For God knows that when you eat of it your eyes will be opened, and you will be like God, knowing good and evil."). Religion insinuates that his revealed word is not complete enough for humanity to live life as God intended, thus requiring humanity to provide the additional necessary information, creating a platform for religion.

The goal is for God's people, Christ's church, to wean ourselves away from the bondage of religion, regardless of how it has been expressed as a tradition, a denomination, or a movement; and to forge ahead, taking his timeless truth grounded in revelation and applying it to the ever-changing world around us. This is the steadfast faith that the church must have to confront an increasingly godless and hostile environment in the years to come. Because of our carnal nature, which continually draws us to humanism, all of our Christian expressions have been contaminated by religious trappings to varying degrees. Sadly, we tend to create theological systems and establish doctrines and practices to suit our well-meant but often misguided notions. Let us not be of those who tenaciously harness themselves to some ill-fated Christianized, institutionalized expression clouded in religious deception. Let us not be among those "respectable" Christians who will pose no real threat to the "prince of the power of the air" (Eph 2:2), being held captive and given over to our carnal religious desires. Our Lord is now calling his people to become unshackled from religion, to unite and become reconciled in the purity of the faith, and to seek peace among ourselves in joining together in his reclamation

A Call to Unity, Peace, and Purity

of his bride. There is a marvelous "marriage supper of the Lamb" awaiting ahead (Rev 19:9). "Let us rejoice and exult and give him the glory, for the marriage of the Lamb has come, and his Bride has made herself ready" (Rev 19:7).

SECTION 3

A Bit of Background

Why Has the Church Been So Divided?

ALTHOUGH MUCH GOOD CAME from the formative years of the early church, history cannot overlook the fact that the church also began to increasingly syncretize worldly elements of the surrounding culture into doctrine, a practice not unlike Israel (God's people) did in the Old Testament. Fallen humanity, in the attempt to "be like God" (Gen 3:5), forever seemed bent toward taking matters into its own hands rather than trusting in what God says (revelation). Regretfully, the temptation to create religion (religious humanism) has always been with us even until today. There is a continual battle between God's revelation and man's religion, and it is this battle that still rages in dividing the church.

As early as the second century the church began to be contentious over issues of legitimacy and influence from various regions. As the church in Rome began to increase in influence, it also began to syncretize elements of the surrounding culture, resulting in a Romanization of the Western church. Likewise, the church in the East, less under Roman influence, began to syncretize elements of the surrounding culture, resulting in an "oriental" or Eastern church.

Later these developments eventually led to the Great Schism between the Eastern and Western churches in 1054 CE.

In the West, mounting issues regarding the understanding of church authority and abuse came to a crisis, resulting in a call for a reformation of the church. Finally, in 1517 CE Martin Luther was able to mobilize a significant portion of what had become the Roman Catholic Church to demand change. This eventually led to the Reformation, resulting in a further division between the Roman Catholic Church and what would become the Western Protestant church. Added to this, the lack of a unified understanding of what was to be "reformed" led to further splits within Protestantism. Nevertheless, from the Reformation, five "solas" emerged as the heartbeat of the movement. These were:

- *Sola gratia* (grace alone—Eph 2:8-9)
- *Sola fide* (faith alone—Eph 2:8-9)
- *Solus Christus* (Christ alone—Heb 4:15)
- *Sola scriptura* (Scripture alone—2 Tim 3:16-17; 2 Pet 1:20-21)
- *Soli Deo gloria* (To God alone be glory—1 Cor 10:31)

It was from these five declarations that the Roman Catholic Church would be challenged. Without question, the most offensive "sola" to the authority of the Roman Catholic Church was to be that of sola scriptura, which proclaims that the final authority of church doctrine would be based upon the Scriptures. This perspective regarding authority, in essence, is the pivotal point between what might be understood as the Christian faith in contrast to that of the Christian religion. The Christian faith is essentially grounded in theism while the Christian religion is essentially grounded in humanism. The perspective of the Christian faith rightly understands that humans can never speak infallibly, as only God is infallible. Humans, unlike God, are limited, while nevertheless continually striving to be faithful to the infallible One. While not denying that much can be gained from church history and tradition, in the end, the Christian faith holds that the Scriptures alone ultimately determine what is to be considered as true regarding the Christian faith. It would be by the word of God that Christ would sanctify his church, "as Christ loved the church and gave himself up for her, that he might sanctify her, having cleansed her by the washing of water with the word, so that he might present the church to himself in splendor, without spot or wrinkle or any such thing, that she might be holy and without blemish" (Eph 5:25–27).

The Latin phrase *Ecclesia reformata, semper reformanda, secundum verbum Dei* (the church reformed, and continuing to be reformed, according to the word of God) has sometimes been described as the central focus of the Reformation. This perspective emphasizes that the effects of the fall necessitate the church continually needing purification until the return of Christ (Eph 5:27; 2 Cor 11:2; Phil 1:10; Titus 2:14; Rev 19:8).

Those of the Christian religion may protest that the infallible Scriptures demand an infallible interpreter, as God would have never given his people his infallible word without some entity that could interpret his word infallibly. Thus, there must be some special human or elite clerical community who would be able to interpret the Scriptures infallibly. The counter to this argument is that God gave his people his infallible word so that his people must continually remain humble in their limitedness, ever resisting the temptation to exalt themselves to be "like God" by claiming any notion of infallibility. God's people must submit themselves to him, ever depending upon him to guide them in interpreting his word faithfully, however, not infallibly, ever reminding themselves of their incapability of doing so in a fallen world. Therefore, holding humans, in any way, to be infallible in what they are capable of doing would reflect the "garden problem" by suggesting that humanity could in any sense obtain any attributes of God restricted to him alone. Furthermore, this would prevent humans from claiming the authority to develop infallible doctrines or traditions equivalent to the authority of the Scriptures, possibly becoming guilty of adding to or subtracting from what God has proclaimed (Deut 12:32; Prov 30:5–6; Rev 22:18–19).

Even so, this is not to mean that his people would be left to themselves to interpret the Scriptures in any fashion they would like, therefore having no credible basis for interpretation. Instead, this would necessitate that God's people as a community must be taught how to faithfully interpret the Scriptures according to sound principles of hermeneutics.

Sadly, God's people in the Old Testament found themselves in such a situation that over the years the clerical class sought increasing authority within a faith that had been eroded greatly by human religiosity. The Jewish people came to falsely believe that because they were God's chosen people, they could not truly go off the rails. The clerical elite, blinded by their pride, exalted themselves in such a way as to believe that they could act with the authority of God by developing rules and traditions beyond what God had plainly given to his people. The result was Judaism, a counterfeit of the original faith that God had given to his people. In the end, this clergy class of Judaism, assuming that they were acting on God's behalf, sought to crucify the very Son of God. Christians of today must learn from history and not be deceived by those who declare that they can act infallibly as God's representatives.

We must never forget that we still live in an ongoing spiritual battle with the world, the flesh, and the devil that began long ago in the garden. The apostle John reminds us that in this world it is the desires of our flesh, the desires of our eyes, and the pride of life that so strongly beset us (1 John 2:16). Likewise, the apostle Peter warns us (1 Pet 5:8) that Satan continues to pursue us as a roaring lion seeking to devour us by every kind of religious deception from his smorgasbord of counterfeits on offer. Again, it is the apostle Paul's urging for us to put on the whole armor of God so that we will be able to stand against the schemes of the devil (Eph 6:10–17). This armor consists of his truth and righteousness along with the gospel of peace, our faith, and the assurance of our salvation as our defense as we march forward with the word of God as our weapon against Satanic attack. It is on the question of whether we give in to religion or hold fast to revelation that the future balance of the church will hang.

A Bit of Background

Seven Destructive Developments of the Early Church

Often there have been what some have called the "sevens" of the church. Most of us are familiar with the seven sins—lust, gluttony, greed, sloth, wrath, envy, and pride—along with the seven virtues: the cardinal virtues of prudence, justice, temperance, and courage (or fortitude) coupled with the theological virtues of faith, hope, and charity. In this same vein, what is being proposed here may be described as the "seven destructive developments" of the early church (from Pentecost until 500 CE). These are: ecclesiastical institutionalism, elitism, authoritarianism, sacerdotalism, mysticism and mystical materialism, asceticism, and monasticism. While it is certain that some would fervently contest whether these developments were destructive, history clearly demonstrates that these seminal notions have proven to be some of the most divisive within the body of Christ.

Ecclesiastical Institutionalism

Beware of the leaven of the Pharisees.

Luke 12:1

It is quite understandable that when trying to find a structure for organizing a body of people the temptation toward institutionalization can often become very enticing. After all, the more one becomes institutionalized, the more secure one may feel. Those of us who have ever worked or lived in a more confined environment such as a military base or a medical compound or even on an academic campus can certainly acknowledge how these types of environments can lend a sense of security. One can even form a sense of identity associated with such environments. In psychological terminology, those who find themselves greatly gravitating toward becoming overly dependent upon being in such settings are often described as becoming "institutionalized"; sometimes, to the point of finding it difficult to function outside of these settings. In a sense, these people have become "captivated" by the institutional system. Admittedly, those who greatly invest themselves in such environments and become highly indoctrinated with certain values, practices, or beliefs may become increasingly less open to any outside or opposing input, often seeing such as threatening to their security and identity. The most infamous extremes of such institutionalization can be found in numerous isolated cults operating throughout the globe.

As a body, the church initially may have been understood to be an "institution," but only with a very small "i" in the same way that a family as a system is likewise organized as an institution. The original organization of God's people was that of a spiritual "family," which is fundamentally organic in nature and not to be patterned after some highly governed hierarchical body. From her inception, the church was composed of small, intimate groups of people who shared life together and were accountable to one another. This understanding harkens back to God's people in the Old Testament who were organized primarily by biological family systems of believers coming together in community and adding to their number with those who were coming into the faith. Leadership in these communities was representative and conciliar.

Regretfully, as the early church became more organized and publicly recognized and accepted, there was an increasing tendency to institutionalize the church, much like the institutions of power in the surrounding culture. This developing tendency of depicting the church as an institution, alongside that of, for example, the institutions of the government or the military, completely distorted the original understanding of who the church was. As a result, the church became highly politicized and at times operated as a serious power broker in determining the course of nations. Added to this, the church accumulated great material wealth and property. In time, the church steadily rose to dominate the overarching psyche in almost every aspect of common life. Finally, the church, now as a powerful institution in society, became a controlling force even to the point of laying claim to each person's eternal destiny. Religious leaders appointed from above by their own elite hierarchy often became the new Pharisees of the emerging church. Eventually, the church became more identified with outward expressions, such as buildings, vestments, rituals, artwork, music, etc., than with real people living real lives. The original understanding of the church increasingly took a backseat to an external religious façade.

Elitism

... not domineering over those in your charge, but being examples to the flock.

1 Peter 5:3

One of the most contentiously debated passages of the New Testament is Matt 16:13–20, where Peter confesses Jesus as the Christ. Many have been curious as to the real intentions of the clerical elite in choosing this passage to be such a matter of theological discourse. How this passage has been approached by various theologians is one of the most outstanding examples for demonstrating what may be called an *eisegesis* (a "reading in") rather than an *exegesis* (a "drawing out") of the meaning of a passage. The prevailing suspicion is that those who have been overly invested in the issue of ecclesiastical legitimacy, authority, or power utilize this passage to read in a preconceived assumption to press their case rather than to correctly understand the actual context of the passage: that is, the truth claim of this passage that focuses on who Jesus is rather than who the apostles were and who Peter was. Furthermore, this passage does not address the office of bishop (not quite yet in the picture of church history) or any other ecclesiastical or clerical matter. The direct question of the passage is whether Jesus is recognized as "the Christ, the Son of the living God" (Matt 16:16). The matter at hand is that Jesus is God, who forever is described in the Old Testament as the Rock (Deut 32:4; 2 Sam 22:2–3; Ps 18:2, 89:26, 95:1; Isa 17:10). It has become more than scandalous regarding how theologians have become completely sidetracked and even obsessed in focusing on the person of Peter, let alone arguing over the meaning of his name, or even referring to any of the apostles in and of themselves as becoming the rock of the church.

Again, it is humanism that drives so many to focus on the elevation of sinful man rather than to focus on God alone. The foundation of the church can never be grounded in any mere mortal but only upon he who is sinless, a flawless foundation. The church is established upon the fact that Jesus is God, the solid Rock, who reconciles man to God. This understanding is the very essence of the entire passage. How tragic is the day to observe where even such plain common sense in understanding Scripture seems to elude the minds of theologians, causing them to stray so much off the mark. Why any Christian could be contentious over such a plain passage of Scripture is certainly a mystery.

The "keys" of the kingdom is this glorious truth, the gospel, that Christ's followers are privileged to proclaim to all of humanity, which will result in either their eternal freedom or captivity. This truth is why Jesus came into the world. This is about his kingdom, which is not a kingdom of this world, not even a religious kingdom of this world. Furthermore, the notion of establishing a religious empire with a clerical nobility is completely foreign to Matthew or any writer of the New Testament.

Even so, man, with his seemingly unending lust for power and control, would find any scheme to justify its attainment. Later, when the concept of bishop (*episkopos*, Gk.) was originally introduced into the church as one serving as an elder (*presbuteros*, Gk.), having oversight among the elders of several churches, this was not to be some royal "blue blood" overlord appointed along some "spiritual bloodline" traced directly back to the apostles themselves. Such a monarchical concept was not in the mind of the first-century church. A bishop was vetted as holding to the faith and teaching of the apostles. It was the content of what the apostles stood for that mattered in one becoming an elder or bishop rather than their belonging to some sort of spiritual bloodline or pedigree. Sadly, it was this misguided understanding of church officers as belonging to some spiritual royal lineage that produced a class

A Bit of Background

system within the church that became exacerbated as elders were relabeled as "priests," resulting in a clergy/laity class split. While the Eastern/oriental church balked at the Roman monarchical interpretation and chose rather a more conciliar structure; still, it nevertheless faltered by backing a similarly false notion of apostolic succession. It is heartbreaking that such a pernicious notion as it has evolved over the past two millennia has proven to be so devastating to the Christian witness.

Authoritarianism

They have rejected me from being king over them.

1 Samuel 8:7

Any student of comparative governmental systems understands that governments, like all things, have familiar dynamics of form vs. freedom, unity vs. diversity, community vs. individuality, etc. These dynamics can often be expressed in governmental systems ranging from highly autocratic to highly democratic systems. Pre-fallen man, being created in the image of God, with him as their King, naturally embraced his need for someone or something to have authority in his life to give him direction. Sadly, fallen man, in rejecting God, began to promote himself or someone other than God to be the "king" of his or her life. As has been said, everyone serves someone. Of course, God plainly stated that no human is designed to bear such authority. We find this in the story of Samuel (1 Sam 8–12), where Israel began doing what was "right in their own eyes" (i.e., people declaring themselves to be king of their own lives), leading to societal chaos with no king outside of themselves to rule them (Judg 21:25).

However, instead of returning to God as their rightful King, Israel turned to the ways of the world around them to solve their problem by desiring a king like other nations. Indeed, a very poor choice. Yet, God, knowing beforehand that Israel would choose this direction, accommodated Israel, allowing them to have a "king like other nations" (1 Sam 8:5). Sadly, this choice would be a disaster in that for the following half millennium God's people would hardly have a handful of kings who were worthy of any honourable mention—David, who was both a murderer and an adulterer, being the best of the lot. Yet, in the irony of it all, God would establish a covenant with David and his lineage which would one day provide God's people once again with their true King (God) in Jesus Christ. Sadly, the world since its conception has suffered horribly at the hands of autocratic rulers (even from "good kings") seeking more power and covering the earth with blood. This is not to say that other types of governments have not done evil, but the lion's share of evil has without question been under autocratic human rule. Even for those autocratic rulers who in times past have tried to faithfully serve God, it is a most difficult struggle with a system that allows them such great power. It is no wonder God particularly warned his people against this type of governance.

Moreover, autocratic systems tend toward elitism, creating ruling classes, such as nobility, and less privileged common classes of people. It is not that other governmental systems exist without people who may personally hold some degree of class consciousness. The problem is that autocratic systems have a built-in bias that is endemic to the system itself, making it difficult to hold all people as being created equal regarding their intrinsic worth before God.

The early church of the Greco-Roman world existed within a culture drenched in autocratic rule—a world of mighty kings and emperors. It is quite understandable that the temptation to legitimize and protect the Christian faith under such a system would be very strong. No doubt, setting up a system of ecclesiastical monarchism through claims of an apostolic succession would be quite appealing. Needless to say, the opposite notion of unbridled democracy and the high individualism of the Western twenty-first century would likewise have been a rather foreign notion to the culture of this era.

However, even more disturbing in this tendency toward church authoritarianism was the notion of the clerical elite being somehow endowed with the sole authority to interpret the word of God even to the point of being able to make "infallible" proclamations outside of Scripture. In time, as the general population gained less personal access to the Scriptures, they became increasingly dependent upon the clerical elite regarding their understanding of the Christian faith. As a result, the clerical elite had less and less accountability from a biblically informed populace, thus giving themselves a rather free hand to rule as they saw fit. Eventually, people began to be indoctrinated by the elite clergy even to the point of believing that when the elite clergy spoke, God spoke. Such a grab for power by the clergy was, without question, the pinnacle of religious humanism.

Now, aware of having made a great many people very unhappy in what has been described as a well-intended but largely man-made worldly system of church authority as it evolved throughout early church history, I am not suggesting that the church does not have a system of governance endorsed by God. Thankfully, since the earliest days of recorded history, our Lord has supported a system of government that avoids the extremes of authoritarianism as well as unfettered democracy.

Sacerdotalism

It is finished.

JOHN 19:30

The apostolic faith of the church in the New Testament is a faith that is "faithful" to the teachings of the apostles as found in the divine revelation of the Scriptures. There is no notion in the Scriptures of a worldly line of succession of an elite clergy class stemming from the apostles. Furthermore, there is no notion of establishing some sort of "Christianized" religious kingdom or empire on this earth ruled by an elite priestly class. The word "priest" (*hiereus*, Gk., or *kohen*, Heb.), denoting an office in the church, has no place in the New Testament. This misnomer is found only in later Latin translations, where "priest" (*sacerdos*, Lat.) is ascribed to the biblical office of elder (*presbuteros*, Gk.). The basic reason that the New Testament writers purposely did not use *hiereus* or "priest" for the office of elder is fundamental to the Christian faith. A priest, *hiereus* or *sacerdos*, in the Old Testament, presided over the administration of a sacrifice, thus referring to a sacrificial system or a "sacerdotal system." The fundamental good news of the gospel is that Christ, the final high priest, administered himself on the altar of the cross as the final sacrifice. There was no further sacrifice, nor further representation of a sacrifice, necessary. Christ himself summed this up in his final three words on the cross that have echoed throughout the ages—"It is finished" (John 19:30).

Therefore, reinstituting a sacerdotal system into the church, requiring a priest, makes a complete mockery of Christ's ultimate sacrifice. Even worse, the later latinized redefining of "elder" to "priest" to fit the reintroduction of the notion of a sacerdotal system of the Eucharist (Lord's Supper) by influential leaders in the early church hugely misrepresents the great mystery of the Eucharist as that which is focused not on a sacrificial meal or a representation of a sacrifice, but on thanksgiving, a celebration, in remembrance of the finished work of Christ on the cross and in his resurrection. As such, the reinstatement of a priestly office has no place in Christianity. The only legitimate priests in Christianity are Christians themselves as they present themselves continually as a "living" sacrifice to God (Rom 12:1; 1 Pet 2:5). Therefore, the usage of an altar in Christian worship is unfounded. If any furnishings in Christian worship are to be utilized, it is the Lord's table of communion that would now be legitimate.

Mysticism and Mystical Materialism

Have nothing to do with irreverent, silly myths.

1 Timothy 4:7

A Bit of Background

Mysticism is a long-held practice whereby one commonly seeks a type of religious ecstasy, often in the desire to become "one with God" or with some sort of Absolute, and is considered to be an exalted level of experience to be pursued. Mysticism is highly subjective, sometimes even producing an altered state of consciousness in being "caught up" in the notion of "mystery." Certainly, the Christian faith contains aspects of mystery—concepts that will never be fully grasped or explained, such as the Trinity, the incarnation, creation, salvation, etc.—and therefore may be described as holding a "mystical" quality; but this is a far cry from seeking esoteric experiences or being "caught up" or consumed by mysticism. While there are those in the Bible who at times found themselves experiencing dreams or visions from God, there are no examples in the Scriptures of God's people who made it a practice of seeking altered states of consciousness or of "losing oneself" in the practice of mysticism. This is not to say that the Christian life is merely that of scholasticism or "cognitive behavioral" Christianity that is devoid of an experiential and supernatural faith. The Christian's entire existence and worship involves a supernatural God. However, seeking an altered state of consciousness untethered from divine revelation found in the Scriptures can become a conduit for satanic deception and false notions. The Scriptures call us to maintain a sound and sober mind (Col 2:18; 1 Tim 3:2; 2 Tim 1:7; Titus 2:2).

Related to mysticism is mystical materialism, whereby a material object may hold some sense of efficacy, energy, force, or power in and of itself. It is a notion closely related to that of animism. The attraction to mystical materialism stems from the belief that one can attain some benefit, whether in healing, assistance, blessing, etc., from an object. Often, it is in such a visible, tangible, or concrete object that many seek to find some assurance that their faith or belief is "real." While such a notion can be readily found in pagan belief systems throughout the world, such a notion as normative to the faith of God's people has no Scriptural support.

One may find isolated instances where God chose to use a material object, such as Moses's staff (Exod 21:8–9) or handkerchiefs

A Call to Unity, Peace, and Purity

(Acts 19:11–12), to bring an effect. Certainly, in the Old Testament God temporarily used a sacrificial system of animals or other tangible offerings as a concrete foreshadowing of the final sacrifice of Christ. However, the notion of people placing their faith in objects rather than in God brings about an understanding that borders on idolatry. Even the use of water in baptism or bread and wine in Communion is not to be understood as placing one's faith in the objects themselves to bring about an effect. Such material objects are utilized only to signify something beyond the object. The object of our faith is not the object itself but God.

Regretfully, the notion of mystical materialism eventually found its way into the church. Church leaders began to promote the use of objects as channels of God's blessing. This is found in the veneration of holy relics, holy water, the concept of baptismal regeneration, transubstantiation, misuse of imagery, and many other practices that would be foreign to the teachings of the Christian faith as found in the word of God.

Asceticism

Some will depart from the faith by devoting themselves to deceitful spirits and teachings of demons, through the insincerity of liars whose consciences are seared, who forbid marriage and require abstinence from foods.

1 Timothy 4:1–3

The notion of asceticism was common to the minds of those who lived in the Greco-Roman world. To some, this meant a simple, minimalistic lifestyle; to others, this could be bodily mortification, habitual self-infliction of pain, and even self-martyrdom. While Jesus and John the Baptist may have chosen to live a rather simple lifestyle, this did not mean that they promoted a rejection of the material world or human pleasure. Jesus, as God, created the material world and created humanity to enjoy pleasure, declaring these

A Bit of Background

as "good." Sadly, fallen humanity tends to twist what God has made and misrepresent his purposes for his creation.

Throughout church history, Christians have struggled with asceticism. The common practice of asceticism was characterized by abstinence from sensual pleasures, often to pursue some spiritual goal. This might take the form of renunciation of material possessions and physical pleasures, possibly to spend more time in fasting, prayer, meditation, and reflection. Often, in everyday life, this translated into sensual inhibition, particularly regarding sexuality, and the exaltation of celibacy. Early church fathers often struggled with asceticism, varying widely in their interpretation of the Scriptures in the light of the culture around them. Such examples can be found in Origen, Jerome, Ignatius, John Chrysostom, and Augustine.

Sexuality often appeared to be extremely troublesome for many of those in the early church and has too often been misrepresented throughout most of Christian history as well. To be sure, one could certainly attest that the worst place to learn about matters of sexuality is from the secular world. However, one might also hold that the second worst place to learn about these matters has too often been within the church. Just hear a sampling of the voices of some of our most respected leaders in church history:

- Justin Martyr (100–165 CE): "We Christians marry only to produce children."[8]
- Clement of Alexandria (150–215 CE): "If a man marries in order to have children, he ought not to have sexual desire for his wife. He ought to produce children by a reverent, disciplined act of the will."[9]
- Tertullian (150–230 CE), regarding women: "Do you not know that you are each an Eve? . . . You are the Devil's gateway."[10]
- Jerome (347–420 CE): "Matrimony is always a vice"; "Do you imagine that we approve of any sexual intercourse except for the procreation of children? He who is too ardent a lover of his own wife is an adulterer"; "Woman is the root of all evil."[11]

- Augustine (354–430 CE): "In Eden, it would have been possible to beget offspring without lust. The sexual organs would have been stimulated into necessary activity by willpower alone, just as the will controls other organs. Then, without being goaded on by the allurement of passion, the husband could have relaxed upon his wife's breasts with complete peace of mind and bodily tranquillity, that part of his body not activated by tumultuous passion, but brought into service by the deliberate use of power when the need arose, the seed dispatched into the womb with no loss of his wife's virginity. So, the two sexes could have come together for impregnation and conception by an act of will, rather than by lustful cravings."[12]

- Augustine, in a letter to a friend: "I fail to see what use woman can be to man, if one excludes the function of bearing children."[13]

- Thomas Aquinas (1225–1274 CE): "As regards the individual nature, woman is defective and misbegotten."[14]

Robert T. Francoeur, a Catholic priest and a fellow of the Society for the Scientific Study of Sex and professor of human embryology and sexuality at Fairleigh Dickinson University summarizes how Christianity became so negative regarding marriage and sexuality:

> To understand the evolution from the early sex-affirming Hebraic culture to Christianity's persistent discomfort with sex and pleasure, we have to look at three interwoven threads: the dualistic cosmology of Plato [i.e. the soul and mind are at war with the body], the Stoic philosophy of early Greco-Roman culture [i.e., nothing should be done for the sake of pleasure], and the Persian Gnostic tradition [i.e., that demons created the world, sex and your body—in which your soul is trapped, and the key to salvation is to free the spirit from the bondage of the body by denying the flesh].

A Bit of Background

> Within three centuries after Jesus, these influences combined to seduce Christian thinkers into a rampant rejection of human sexuality and sexual pleasure.[15]

No wonder Christians have too often been the target of many jokes regarding sexuality. While it would be completely unfair to suggest that all early church leaders were negative on marriage and sexuality, one must admit that the overall tone set by many early leaders cast a rather dim view of these matters among the people of God. Even with the increased embracing of sexuality over the past century by Christians, there is still much work to be done.

Thankfully, as always, one must again simply refer to the Scriptures to gain a proper understanding of marriage and sexuality. Regard the following:

- Marriage and the sexual relationship were part of creation itself—"Therefore a man shall leave his father and his mother and hold fast to his wife, and they shall become one flesh" (Gen 2:24).
- Proverbs describes finding a wife as a blessing (Prov 5:18–19; 18:22).
- The Song of Solomon is a beautiful description of marital sexual love.
- The apostle Paul, addressing the church at Corinth, calls for people to marry to avoid sexual temptation (1 Cor 7:2).
- Marriage is depicted as being compared to Christ's relationship to the church (Eph 5:22–33).
- In holding a church office, being married is endorsed (if not required) (1 Tim 3:2; 12; Titus 1:6).
- Finally, in Revelation, we find at the consummation of all things, the marriage supper of the Lamb to his bride, the church (Rev 19:6–9).

From the Scriptures, we find that sexuality is a part of all human existence, whether one is single or married. Marriage and the bearing of children are mandated in God's creative design as being good. That the church could have ever come to the notion of measuring one's spirituality or ability to serve in all of Christ's church based upon being more or less sexual as a human being certainly ranks high in theological absurdity. Such an understanding has no basis in the whole counsel of the Scriptures. Only when snippets of biblical texts are taken out of context can one draw any other conclusion. Asceticism is humanistic and worldly to the core, regardless of how Christians have justified it in the past. In the apostle Paul's letter to the Colossians, he particularly warned against the temptation toward asceticism (Col 2:18 and 2:23).

Monasticism

*I do not ask that you take them out of the world,
but that you keep them from the evil one.*

JOHN 17:15

A logical extension of asceticism is that of monasticism, often depicted by living as a hermit or cloistered, being labeled as "religious." Typically, as a monastic, one renounces worldly pursuits to devote oneself fully to spiritual work. However, living as a monastic has no basis in the Christian faith as described in the Scriptures. While there were those such as Elijah and John the Baptist who would spend much of their lives in a somewhat nomadic fashion, none were called by God to live as a hermit or to cloister themselves away from normal people. Without question, Jesus intended that his followers be in the world as his witnesses and live life fully integrated within all of God's people. Even the more mendicant orders, such as the Dominicans and Franciscans as well as more recent religious congregations such as the Missionaries of Charity (often identified with Mother Teresa), while involving themselves in the lives of those outside through evangelization and humanitarian relief, still adhere to taking ascetic vows.

Again, it is this concept of being religious by taking vows of self-denial of material possessions or of renunciation of human pleasure (particularly sexual pleasure) that finds its roots in asceticism. Even more distorted is the idea that being religious would have anything to do with being more spiritual or closer to God. Again, this does not mean that one may not temporarily fast or periodically take time away to spend more concentrated time with God. However, this is much different from taking on an existence of isolation from the normal church community or of self-deprivation from normal human pleasure. Such thinking is a total misunderstanding of true spirituality.

Summation

The syncretism of elements such as these into the church created an increasing heterodoxy—a blending of foreign ideas with Christian orthodoxy. This process led to understandings, assumptions, practices, and doctrines that later resulted in confusion and division among the people of God. A merit-based system for justification, purgatory, misuse of imagery, and an increasing focus upon and exaltation of human beings rather than God alone are such examples of a humanistic shift. Sadly, over the past two millennia, the results of syncretism have gradually resulted in Christians being deceived into thinking of our faith as that of a religion to be held alongside and compared with other religions.

It is generally agreed that when the church begins to look more like the surrounding culture rather than existing within the culture and reflecting a separate distinction from that culture, then something has seriously gone wrong. Likewise, when the church begins to look more like a religion than a way of grasping reality and living out this reality, then something equally serious has taken place.

As one reflects back through history and recounts what happened to God's people in the two thousand years from Abraham until the advent of Christ, it is the accumulation of religion that suffocated the true revelatory faith of the Jews into becoming merely the "Jewish religion" (Judaism). It was this religiosity that blinded the eyes of the Jewish religious leaders to the point that they failed to even recognize the incarnate Son of God and thus sought to exterminate him as a threat to their arrogant pride and religious system.

Could the same not be said of the "Christian religion": that the accumulation of religion over the past millennia since the advent of Christ is also what has suffocated true revelatory faith in Christ? Could well-intending humans' fabrication of a Christianized religious system, eventually resulting in different renditions of traditions, denominations and movements, be the crux of why the church has become so divided? Would it be possible that God's people will someday become more honest with themselves (something with which people have great difficulty) and pursue truth to set them free from the entrapment of religion that has so long plagued Christ's bride?

So now we come to the central point of this manifesto. What is being set forth here is that we all, as believers, have to some measure become deceived by replacing a truly theistic worldview with a humanistic worldview, or what may specifically be described as a Christianized religious humanism. In coming to this realization, everything, yes, *everything*, becomes challenged. Our entire understanding of Christ, the church, the Bible, and even of reality and truth come under a reevaluation. This realization is more than merely upsetting; this realization places us in a crisis of faith and life, far beyond just a mild revolution in our thinking.

Coming into the understanding that our God has never had any interest or investment in religion whatsoever, but that his interest lies ultimately in reality, is quite disturbing, to say the least. If this is true, then what have we been playing at for all these millennia? Even more so, why would our loving heavenly Father allow us to be so deceived? Or maybe, could it be that we have just not been listening? Could the world around us, regardless of time or culture, have been far more of an influence on our understanding and experience than we have been willing to acknowledge? How could our human pride have blinded our eyes or closed our ears to the light or voice of God to such an enormous degree? Ultimately, it is most likely because our fallen humanity is so innately drawn to ourselves and to humanism rather than to God and theism. The call then is to return to a truly theistic worldview, and thus to revelation, as being the source of our reality testing and what the Christian faith entails.

SECTION 4

Hope for the Church

Returning to the Scene of the Crime

IN ISA 11, THE prophet looks to a time when the world will one day be at peace and harmony, which ultimately depicts the longed-for future of Christ's reign. In verse 6 we read "and a little child shall lead them." While various theological interpretations of this passage have been proposed, one thing that stands out is that the portrayal of children throughout the Scriptures often depicts them as those who are either innocent or unsuspecting. Sometimes, when trying to find solutions to seemingly insurmountable problems, it is often the simple, the obvious, that is staring us straight in the face and that we seemingly cannot see. We often search for solutions far more complex than necessary. Certainly, we may gain much from the experts, those highly knowledgeable with several academic degrees behind their names, in assisting us in finding a way forward. And yet, the way forward may be so obvious that even a child can indicate the clearest path.

As has been stated, this manifesto is certainly not one that many of those in academia will readily endorse. It is not heavily undergirded by documentation and elaborate argumentation or set forth as some apologetic. It is purposely intended for the common reader as a rather straightforward call to repentance for the church to cast off the chains of religion and take hold of Christ and his revelation in the hope of aligning his people with Jesus's high priestly prayer (John 17). In doing so, the church must return to the obvious, what even a child can easily point to. We must return to the garden, the scene of the original crime. It is here that we encounter the root cause and can find the answer as to why the church has had so much difficulty in becoming more unified, purer, and more at peace.

Again, it is the "garden problem" that the leaders of the church must see as the fundamental problem under which God's people have suffered. It is the church that has continually been deceived by Satan with the same original confrontation—that is, God cannot be fully trusted in providing his people with credible and sufficient information to live a life pleasing to him. As has been previously stated, we find this basic formula of Satan's deception, leading Eve to doubt God: either (1) to question the credibility of God's word or one's ability to comprehend God's word, or (2) to infer the inadequacy of God's word as not being fully complete or sufficient for one to live in obedience to God, and, thus, in need of amending or of further clarification. This rebellion in doubting God, giving in to the temptation "to be like God," ushered in the fall of man, resulting in the rise of humanism. Regretfully, the chief blame for this worldview becoming syncretized into the life of the church must be ascribed to those leaders who have led God's people astray.

A case has been proposed that one of the most divisive elements in the church today are those expressions that exclusively claim to be the "true church" or the "fullness of the church," thus making all other expressions either irrelevant or minimized. These expressions have historically been held as the guiltiest parties in sowing the seeds of discord among God's people. Again, this stems from a fundamental misunderstanding of the church as being intrinsically institutional rather than organic in nature. An institutional perspective defines the church as being based primarily upon that of form, or the "what" of the church, whereas a biblical perspective defines the church as being based primarily upon that of organic content, or the "who" of the church. Nevertheless, by regaining a proper perspective on the definition of the church, it can be hoped that substantive progress can be made in the coming years.

Division among Christians has been Satan's primary strategy to make the Christian faith a matter of confusion rather than a matter of hope for all of humanity. The solution is to try to rid the people of God from this ongoing conflict. When there is conflict, there needs to be a way forward. Thankfully, the Scriptures (as well as many social scientists) attest to how matters of conflict can be understood and how to deal with such situations.

Sometimes conflict can be handled by *avoidance*. Normally, avoidance of conflict is only recommended as a temporary short-term solution to a potentially threatening situation. Examples may be found in Jesus escaping through the crowd (John 10:39) or the apostle Paul escaping over a wall (Acts 9:23–25). These examples do not reflect cowardice on the part of Jesus or Paul, but rather a temporary way of handling a situation when the time for confrontation was not helpful for the moment.

Another way of handling conflict might be through direct *competition* with an opposing party, fighting for one's position over that of the opposing party. We find such an instance in Acts 15:36–41, where Paul and Barnabas could not reach an agreement regarding whether to take John Mark on their second missionary journey. In the end, the two apostles parted ways, refusing to give in to the demands of the other. Thankfully, the conflict worked itself out, in the end, resulting in two missionary teams being formed, with Paul and John Mark finding themselves eventually reconciled (Col 4:10; 2 Tim 4:11).

Sometimes, the best way to handle conflict is through *accommodation*, where one party simply gives in to the other party. Because of his previous opposition to the Christian faith and attacks upon Christians, the apostle Paul was initially rejected by the church (Acts 9:26–28). However, after hearing the testimony of Barnabas, the church changed her position and welcomed Paul.

Also, there are times when a *compromise* is made. In Acts 15:1–21 the church reached the decision that gentile male believers were not required to be circumcised. Yet, soon thereafter, in Acts 16:1–5, we find Timothy (a gentile believer) agreeing to be circumcised because of his witness before the Jews. While Timothy was not giving up his right not to be circumcised, because of more important matters he compromised this right to be more effective in ministry.

While the above approaches to handling conflict may be utilized given different situations, the most promising way forward in dealing with conflictual matters is through *cooperation*. To effectively cooperate, parties in conflict must look outside of themselves and find a "third way" to work through conflict. One of the best examples of cooperation can be found in Acts 6:1–6, regarding a disagreement over how to address the social concerns of the church. In this situation, some gentile believers were complaining and demanding that the apostles address the practical needs of their widows. The apostles, seeing that their primary ministry was that of teaching the word of God, decided to create the office of deacon to handle the practical needs of the church. In this way, a new creative solution was found to provide for the demands of both parties. Both parties, by trusting one another and investing in looking for a solution beyond merely defending their present positions, discovered a way forward. (See appendix C and appendix D for helpful examples).

Unlike recent ecumenical movements that tend to overlook theological differences for the sake of unity, what I am proposing is a perspective that aligns more with what the heart of Christ's high priestly prayer intends. As previously stated, this perspective is not found by adhering to a particular tradition, denomination, or movement. It is a perspective that seeks not only unity but also the peace and purity of his church. It is the true meaning of "one church." Rather than overlooking theological differences, such a perspective seeks unity founded upon theological truth derived from divine revelation, the Scriptures. Such a perspective holds that the Scriptures are completely reliable and sufficient in establishing doctrine for the faith and life of the Christian. This is the fundamental reason why God gave his people such revelation.

While insight can be gained from non-Scriptural sources that may be supportive in the application of doctrine, doctrine is not to be derived from these sources. It must be noted that Satan, since the garden, has continually tempted God's people and led them astray by telling them that what God says is either inadequate or cannot be rightly understood. There must be something more or something else needed. This is where Satan introduces "truth," appearing as an angel of light (2 Cor 11:14) but in reality being counterfeit, twisting God's truth. This counterfeit is what essentially divides the church. The church's hope lies in identifying what is counterfeit and consequently ridding the church of such error. Opposing parties must cooperate by looking beyond themselves and looking to God for the solution. God has given us his divine revelation, his word (the Logos), as the sufficient foundation for what it is that comprises the Christian faith. While Christ is the human incarnation of the Logos, the Bible is the God-breathed written Logos.

The initial place to start would be by *cultivating a Christian faith perspective* within the church. Such a perspective would be beyond any particular tradition, denomination, or movement and would seriously invest in reclaiming the church from religion and philosophy (both being derived from human imagination) that have so often permeated the community of God's people since the garden. This perspective would be consistent with a truly Christian theistic worldview founded upon the word of God ("Sanctify them in the truth; your word is truth" [John 17:17]). It would be faithful to the Scriptures as verbally inspired by God and inerrant in the original writings, being fully trustworthy in all that is stated, while holding to a historical-grammatical hermeneutic established upon the understanding that in being God's word, the Scriptures are self-interpreting, infallible, and the final authority in governing Christian faith and life (1 Thess 2:13; 2 Tim 3:16; 2 Pet 1:21).

Such a perspective would be committed to "equipping the saints for the work of ministry, for building up the body of Christ, until we all attain to the unity of the faith and the knowledge of the Son of God" (Eph 4:12–13). It would strive, if at all possible, to bring the reclamation of the Christian faith from within one's tradition, denomination, or movement while not readily abandoning one's tradition, denomination, or movement unless there is an undue hardening of hearts against any significant change (e.g., total incompatibility of the new with the old—Matt 9:16–17; Mark 2:21–22; Luke 5:36–39). At the same time, those seeking to reclaim the Christian faith would naturally find themselves increasingly associating with others who are like-minded across all expressions to find mutual encouragement and further dialogue. And finally, by praying for the Holy Spirit to purify the church based upon his revelation, God's people will come to see that any reclamation of the Christian faith is wholly dependent upon him as the "founder and perfecter of our faith" (Heb 12:2).

Secondly, by *restoring the Scriptures to God's people*, such a perspective would treasure the word of God to be held fast in the hearts and minds of the people of God. It is sometimes questioned as to why the Scriptures are so important to the Christian faith. According to the Christian Trinitarian concept of the Godhead, the person of the Father is commonly set forth as the intrinsic nature of the essence of the Godhead, the person of the Son (Logos) as the expression of that essence, and the person of the Holy Spirit as the efficacy of that essence. This is not to be understood as modalism, where God is depicted in three forms, but as one God consisting of three persons, coequal and eternal, having that same essence. While the Son is the living expression of the Godhead who, through the person of Jesus, became human, the Scriptures (the word or Logos) are the written expression of God's divine revelation to his people.

It is through this revelatory truth, in propositional form, that God's people can come to know that which comprises the Christian faith. It is by the Holy Spirit that this divine truth becomes efficacious in our lives. Therefore, it is paramount that God's people have ready access to read and study the Scriptures. They are called to learn in a community wherein they also have accountability.

Such a community would naturally seek to provide resources to be made available for proper study and for gaining a proper hermeneutic (model for interpretation). Finally, they would learn to apply God's word to live the Christian life and as a witness before the watching world.

Thirdly, and perhaps the most important aspect in unifying the church, is *upholding the reliability and sufficiency of the Scriptures*. It must be insisted that the Scriptures alone are reliable and sufficient for determining the doctrines of the Christian faith. Even so, this is not to say that outside information cannot be informative and helpful in applying the Christian faith to everyday life. Nevertheless, it must be held that the primary reason behind God giving his people special or divine revelation is that humans were not intended to determine the authoritative doctrines of the faith. To do so would be slipping into humanism, as humans would seek to share a claim to God's exclusive authority, hence the garden problem. Humanism is expressed in the form of philosophical humanism or religious humanism. Again, "progressives" and "liberals" tend to lean toward philosophical humanism by looking to the world regarding the Scriptures. On the other hand, "traditionalists" and "legalists" may lean toward religious humanism, insisting that God has given humans (i.e., church leaders) the authority to "enrich" the Christian faith by expanding beyond the Scriptures, eventually establishing well-intended traditions that would eventually equal the Scriptures in importance.

This manifesto declares that we should cultivate a common perspective of seeing Christ's church reclaimed beyond the factions that we have created over the past two millennia. Certainly, such a perspective will significantly challenge those who tenaciously place their identity and security in their particular tradition, denomination, or movement. Without a doubt, coming to grips with the fact that there may be more beyond what one has known or experienced, and that the possibility of a more united, peaceful, and pure church can be realized, may be difficult to imagine. Regretfully, it is to be expected that many may find it more comforting to simply retreat into the past.

Hope for the Church

While not intending to be prophetic, it is interesting to note that approximately every half millennium, God seems to bring his people to a highly significant place of reckoning.

For example: (*denoting approximate dates):

- 2081* BCE Abrahamic covenant
- 1446* BCE Mosaic covenant
- 1010* BCE Davidic covenant
- 537* BCE Return from exile/captivity
- 05* BCE Advent of Christ
- 451 CE Chalcedonian Schism
- 1054 CE Great East-West Schism
- 1517 CE Reformation of the church
- 20?? CE Reclamation of the Christian faith and reconciliation of the church

Could it be possible, that in this new millennium, God could be bringing his people together in a reconciliation of his church? Could it be that people are finally so weary and disheartened regarding the divisions among us that we would be willing to bring everything and place it on the table for an honest discussion? Could the theological elite among us humble themselves to the point of turning over their particular reins of power and lay all of it at the foot of the cross? Could people ever come to find their real identity and security in Christ as far greater in importance than their particular tradition, denomination, or movement? How long do we, the people of God, have to continually suffer division at the hands of man?

So, what could Christ be trying to do with his church now that it has been two thousand years since his advent here on earth? Certainly, there must be some plan. Thankfully, there is a plan. As hinted at earlier, we find his plan in Eph 5:25–27, where Christ is seeking to sanctify his church:

A Call to Unity, Peace, and Purity

> Christ loved the church and gave himself up for her, that he might sanctify her, having cleansed her by the washing of water with the word, so that he might present the church to himself in splendor, without spot or wrinkle or any such thing, that she might be holy and without blemish.

Christ is in the process of purifying his church. How is he doing this? By his word. He is calling his people to break free from the captivity of religion and seek freedom through his revelation as found in the Scriptures. In Titus 2:14 this concept of Christ "purifying" his church is further emphasized as being under his redemptive plan.

In recent years, as I travel across the globe, I continually sense a yearning of God's people—regardless of denomination, tradition, or movement—toward somehow finding a way forward in overcoming the divisions among us, yet without relinquishing truth. Years ago, when most Christians had almost given up on the possibility of any global change ever taking place within the universal church, many witnessed what has been called the "charismatic movement." Although, no doubt, there have been many legitimate theological and psychological concerns about numerous aspects of such a movement, nevertheless, it cannot be denied that something was happening that transcended denominational boundaries throughout the world and gave hope to many that Christ could truly unite the church. It is from observing this phenomenon that many realized that it could certainly be possible for the Spirit of God to move in such a way that his people could be affected globally. And, if God is in the business of seeking to purify his church, then neither denominations nor traditions will ever be able to prevent this from happening.

Honestly, it would be thrilling to one day be able to find rest in simply being a "Christian" without having to specify anything else—Baptist, Lutheran, Methodist, Catholic, Anglican, Presbyterian, Reformed, evangelical, Orthodox, Pentecostal, charismatic—whatever. While it is quite doubtful that this generation will see any major shift, it would be this hope that many today would like to leave to their children, grandchildren, and the generations to come. Divisions have been continuously caused by those on both ends of the spectrum—those who continually divide the church by picking the church apart and splitting hairs over every minute issue as well as those who divide the church by stubbornly holding to their particular tradition or denomination exclusively as the "true church." We must always keep in mind that in the Scriptures our Lord never called anyone to establish a particular tradition or denomination. He saw his church as being one body. How can we ever hope to move forward and be a part of the solution and not remain a part of the problem? How can we seek peace and unity while also joining others in the sanctification of his church? Certainly, only by humility, repentance, prayer, and seeking his face (2 Chr 7:14).

Reconciliation and Reclamation of the Family

Since time began, humanity has consistently been led back to the connection between faith and family in God's economy regarding how he has ordered this world. Why do social scientists repeatedly acknowledge how the family is the building block of society—as it is often stated, "so goes the family, so goes society"? And by family, I refer not to the relatively recent definition of family as the "nuclear" family, consisting of only parents and children, but to the historical family as it has been expressed across all cultures and within the context of the Scriptures, which today is often called the "extended" family, consisting of grandparents, grandchildren, uncles and aunts, cousins, and in-laws. It is this larger family that has always been the foundation of society in that merely a nuclear family could never fulfill all that is required from a supportive network.

While the smaller husband-wife-child unit would certainly have particular dynamics as a man and woman would "leave and cleave," this would not reflect an alienation from the larger family system. A nuclear family structure would have been considered merely a small fragment of what a family would entail. "The term *nuclear family* first appeared in the early 20th century. The American dictionary Merriam-Webster dates the term back to 1924, and the British *Oxford English Dictionary* has a reference to the term from 1925; thus the term is relatively new."[16] The term gradually came to define a typical family paralleling the rise of industrialization, urbanization, and individualism, particularly in the West, where people leave extended family systems, residing in more rural and small-town communities as a response to the changing economic landscape and vocational opportunities found in cities. Moreover, the norm of the extended family found in cities in earlier times also changed significantly with industrialization, where work and home life became increasingly separate worlds.

Adding to this trend, young adults of recent years might be described as the "friends" generation, heavily influenced by television sitcoms such as *Seinfeld*, *Friends*, and *The Big Bang Theory*. These television programs, although admittedly quite humorous, model adulthood as a community of notoriously immature and dysfunctional individuals stumbling along trying to find their way in life. Any notion of belonging to an extended biological family system is minimal at best and more often completely absent. The clear message is that for adults, friends are more important to life than family.

Sadly, because so many modern families of such individuals have become so dysfunctional and weak in influence, these friends have often come to replace the biological family. This is not to say that having friends is in any way a bad thing. The Scriptures attest to how having solid friends can be a blessing (Prov 27:6, 9–10). Even so, in no way do the Scriptures ever teach that biological families are to be minimized or replaced in importance by friends. The biological family is designed by God as the foundation of social order and integral to the church. Even well-meaning Christians have at times misinterpreted the Scriptures in such a manner as to present Jesus as being somehow demeaning of the biological family and only prioritizing the spiritual family of believers. This is far from what Jesus would ever suggest. We must remember that Jesus was God incarnate and as God, he created the biological family by design as foundational to all of life. By Jesus deliberately comparing one's love for him as needing to exceed one's love for one's biological family, he was reinforcing the importance of the biological family and one's love for it. Only one's love for God himself was to exceed this love. All believers, including those in the biological family, join together to form an eternal spiritual family.

Furthermore, it is important to note that marriage throughout most of human history was never just an individual affair. It was always a matter of uniting biological families, whether a marriage was prearranged or not. The very worst insult, not to mention a great dishonor, would be for two individuals to come together and then somehow independently announce to their families that they were getting married. In many cultures, this would not only be unthinkable but would incur great wrath and a probable penalty from both families as well as the entire community. Marriage, representing both families, stressed the importance of a union in passing down the very essence and testimony of all they would hold dear and for which the two families stood. Even throughout biblical history, marriage was completely a matter between families, and even though it is a covenantal relationship founded by God, marriage was, in fact, originally celebrated as a civil ceremony. In the Western world, the marriage ceremony did not even include a clergy member until 1184 CE when the Council or Synod of Verona made marriage a sacrament in which a priest was to be present. Later, in 1563 CE, the Council of Trent added the requirement of a priest and two witnesses. Only in the sixteenth century was a marriage ceremony allowed to be held inside a church building.

Even though the importance of family did not negate the importance of the individual, any honorable individual would define themselves within the context of their family. Any two individuals contemplating marriage would never conceive of embarking on such a course without the full support and involvement of family from the very beginning of the relationship and throughout the course of their lives. Adults "leaving and cleaving" in establishing themselves as a separate unit was never to be understood as necessarily moving any great distance geographically, as the larger family system was both an economic and social community. Furthermore, this would never mean an emotional cutoff, nor any sense of alienation between the couple and their families of origin. The marital couple growing up in Christian families would continue to honor their parents by living their lives in obedience to the beliefs and values on which their parents raised them and passing these on to their children. The apostle Paul even depicted an "evil generation" as comprising adults who were "disobedient to parents" (Rom 1:30; 2 Tim 3:2). Indeed, it was the larger family system that was to be the primary instrument in preserving the Christian faith as commonly shared with the larger Christian community, Christ's church.

Reconciliation and Reclamation of Community

Over the past century, people have genuinely suffered greatly because of the increasing deficit of truly belonging to an intimate community of people. Much of this has been due to the continual geographic displacement of people, often because of changing economic and vocational demands. However, this has also been exacerbated by an inordinate overemphasis on the individual at the expense of all else. There was once a time when an individual would choose a vocation based upon the impact the vocational choice would have on the family, realizing that certain vocations might separate them from the larger family system or that the vocation in and of itself was not family friendly.

Today it has almost become commonplace to disregard the larger family system when deciding upon a vocation. Sadly, much of Christianity has also largely succumbed to the thinking of this world. Vocational choice has become highly individualistic, where the only criteria of choice are for each person to reach their potential, regardless of anything or anyone else. Even when one is uniquely gifted for a certain vocation, often how this is to be fulfilled is encouraged from quite an individualistic perspective, rather than from the perspective of how this fulfillment can be accomplished in the light of the larger family or surrounding community.

Furthermore, a matter of increasing concern is the formation of the future generation. How will our children and grandchildren be raised and educated? What will they need to know and how will they relate to the world around them, especially as this world becomes increasingly less Christian and where the church is depicted as being irrelevant to society as a whole? Nevertheless, this problem is certainly not new. Even eighteenth-century Christian social activist William Wilberforce shared this common concern:

> I hope you don't think I am being arrogant or overly harsh on cultural Christians. Look at the facts. Do cultural Christians view the Christian faith as important enough to make a priority when teaching their children what they believe and why they believe it? Or do they place greater emphasis on their children getting a good education than on learning about the things of God? Would they be embarrassed if their children did not possess the former while basically being indifferent about the latter? If their children have any understanding of the Christian faith at all, they probably have acquired it on their own. If the children view themselves as Christians, it is probably not because they have studied the facts and come to a point of intellectual conviction but because their family is Christian, so they believe they must be Christian also. The problem with this way of thinking is that authentic faith cannot be inherited. When Christianity is viewed in this way, intelligent and energetic young men and women will undoubtedly reach a point where they question the truth of Christianity and, when challenged, will abandon this "inherited" faith that they cannot defend. They might begin to associate with peers who are unbelievers. In this company, they will find themselves unable to respond to objections to Christianity with which they are confronted. Had they really known what they believe and why they believe it, these kinds of encounters would not shake their faith one bit.[17]

Wilberforce recognized, that even while living in a time when family and community were more honored and where Christianity was more culturally influential, laying a firm foundation for posterity was necessary. It is without question that in today's environment, it is even more imperative that Christians develop spiritual, economic, and educational communities in contrast to those of the world. Yet, while doing so, we must also continually remember that the church is called to be "salt and light" to the world (Matt 5:13–16) and an agent for godly transformation.

What this means for the Christian community beyond the family is a matter of increasing concern. How do we as a community live in a culture that is less supportive or even antagonistic to the Christian faith? How do we do business? How do we educate? How do we care for one another? And of course, how do we interact with the culture in which we live as being "in the world" but not "of the world"? Will we remove our children from educational institutions that intentionally indoctrinate children with beliefs and values that stand in direct opposition to those of the Christian faith? Will we start our own schools or become homeschoolers? What if such schools or even homeschooling itself become outlawed as is presently done in some countries? What if Christians are discriminated against in being employed? Do we start our own businesses? What about where we live and the high cost of housing? What if we find ourselves as a people of God needing to purchase large sections of land and build our own communities? Will normal Christians come to one day find themselves depicted by the world as being some sort of religious cult? Will Christians find themselves living as they once did in the days of the early church, being considered "outcasts" in a world in which they once considered themselves as being "normal"? These are just some of the challenges that could face Christ's bride in the generations ahead.

Reconciliation and Reclamation of the Organized Church

This trend in being a more individualized culture has not left the church unaffected. In times past God's people always dwelt in community with one another, representing a spiritual family. As an increasingly individualized lifestyle has permeated all areas of society, much of local church life today mirrors less interdependence among God's people, where people now generally experience "going to church" as merely an isolated event during the week rather than living in close community with ongoing interaction with one another.

As early as the time of Moses, the leadership structure for God's people was in the hands of elders, adult men in a community chosen by the people to represent them. These elders came from among individual families, family systems, clans, and tribes. These elders held their authority in conciliar groupings, or councils, each being vetted to their office by meeting a particular set of criteria. This governmental structure was representative of the people while not succumbing to an unfettered democratic structure based entirely on peer popularity, and certainly not an autocratic structure reflecting a hierarchical order chosen from within itself and unaccountable to the people. This governmental structure was designed to function as firmly upholding God as the overarching authority from which all governing was to be established: thus, a government grounded in theism.

Regretfully, this structure was later greatly altered as God's people turned from his eldership rule and sought to be like the surrounding world, giving themselves over to monarchism. While God warned his people against doing this, he nevertheless chose to temporarily accommodate their request. Although knowing the disastrous result of such a human autocratic system, nevertheless, he would utilize the system to usher in and restore himself as their true King in the promised Messiah, Jesus Christ. It is with this understanding that the apostles restored God in Christ as their true King under the representative leadership of elders. It is to this structure that the church must return.

Such an eldership structure is one in which God's people nominate those whom they would choose to lead them according to scriptural criteria (1 Tim 3:1–7; Titus 1:5–9). These nominees are then examined by those in leadership holding to the same criteria and then placed before the people for a final decision before the appointment. This similar pattern is found in the Old Testament in the choosing of leaders under Moses (Deut 1:9-18), in the selection of the apostolic successor of Judas (Acts 1:15-26), and in the choosing of deacons (Acts 6:1-6; 1 Tim 1:8-13). This leadership structure thus avoids the extremes of either hierarchical authoritarianism or unfettered democratic popularity contests. Only vetted leaders are chosen by the people. Leaders are accountable to the people and may be removed by the people. Elders serve local communities as well as possibly serving with larger oversight (i.e., as bishops), as attested from early church history. Assisting elders/bishops are those who are called deacons (*diákonos*, Gk., or servant, minister). The office of deacon was established in Acts 6 when the apostles found themselves unable to meet all the practical ministry demands of the local church.

This manifesto is calling upon God's people to rise up and hold all denominations, traditions, and movements to account. God's people deserve far better than the mess that has been made of the church. We need to demand, even to the point of walking out by voting with our feet, a church who would come to realize that the only hope is to start by becoming humble and to move beyond a purely institutional mindset by turning to God's word and rediscovering a church who will aspire to once again be "one, holy, catholic, and apostolic." The church of the Scriptures is neither "Eastern" nor "oriental" nor "Roman" nor "Protestant." Such labels have never been helpful. Even the term "Protestant" was thrust upon those former Catholics who sought reform as a "protest" against many of the doctrines and practices of Roman Catholicism. Luther preferred the German term *evangelisch* (evangelical—derived from *euangelion*, Gk., or good news/gospel) while Calvin preferred either this term or "reformed" (*réformé*, Fr.). Yet, again, we must move beyond such labels. Those from the Eastern/Oriental Orthodox world must come to grips with the fact that they do not own the concept of orthodoxy, as those from Roman Catholicism do not own the concept of catholicity. Likewise, Protestants are not the only evangelicals on the planet.

As has been stated, the first step toward the reclamation and consolidation of God's people is not to just walk away from the particular denomination, tradition, or movement that one may be associated with but rather to attempt to influence one's present community in moving beyond long-held mindsets that only shut down and prevent any progress. Understandably, this will be most difficult among those expressions who stubbornly insist on their group being exclusive in defining themselves as the "true church" in that such exclusive claims, by default, only produce division. Such bodies, tragically, may simply never be able to find any reason whatsoever to ever give up their long-held claims of exclusivity. It may be that such bodies will eventually be left to themselves and suffer their own fate. If one finds oneself in such a situation, it would be strongly suggested that such a person look elsewhere where more hope can be fostered. Satan seeks to allure God's people away from the Christian faith to such expressions as these that only perpetuate disunity. Sadly, many such bodies have become so deeply saturated in religion to the point that they become unable to see that they have played into Satan's deception. Again, any form of a highly institutionalized religion is extremely attractive, especially to those who find themselves drifting in insecurity, trying to find a place to belong or call "home," in the hope of gaining a sense of safety and identity. Alarmingly, our Lord Jesus warns that the dreadful day will come when Satan deceives and leads many astray, if possible even the elect, into following false expressions of the true faith only to find themselves ushering in their own destruction (Matt 24:22–25; Mark 13:20–23).

Some Practical Application

Now, it may be asked, "Well, all of this sounds quite lofty and theoretical, but what can one actually do to help move the church forward?" Without a common worldview as a foundation, little true progress can be made. The following suggestions are offered as ways to "perturb" the present entrenched thinking of so many.

A Call to Unity, Peace, and Purity

First of all, any lasting change must begin within our own minds and hearts. We, ourselves, must become fully convinced that our Lord is calling his church to unity, peace, and purity to the point that we are willing to face some discomforting questions and take a very honest, vulnerable but courageous look at whom we have understood the church to be. If one only sees the church as an exclusive, highly institutionalized organization held together by a rigidly structured governmental elite body, often operationalized by a hierarchical authoritarian system with a plethora of rules and regulations, then this sort of limited understanding will be difficult to overcome.

Such an understanding normally authorizes a great deal of power to those in leadership, and to be candid, those to whom such power is given rarely desire to relinquish this power very easily. Alas, if we gain any lesson from history, it is to be expected that every effort will be made by those in power within such systems to adamantly continue to try to justify and legitimize their particular system. Such systems can be quite deceptive because they offer a seductive sense of certainty and security, such that people willingly turn over power to the system, assuming that any other option would be too hard. It will take those who are willing to courageously search the Scriptures to discover that such an understanding of the church is simply not found in the Bible. While the church can be said to be "institutional" in the sense that she is instituted by Christ as the family is also instituted, the biblical church is fundamentally organic and is likened to that of an intimate family with members serving together responsibly, each with their unique gifts fulfilling particular roles, all being treated with respect and dignity, with each member enjoying a rich relationship with Christ and with one another. Leadership is representative, chosen by the people, lending oversight and being held as examples before others (1 Pet 5:2–3). Local churches are held accountable to one another through conciliar representation in fraternal relationships. It may be that instead of being part of a denomination, churches may seek to establish "fellowship arrangements" with like-minded local churches whereby more intimate fellowship and accountability can be established between churches. A common statement of faith held by these local churches could enable theological unity. (See appendix F).

Furthermore, those desiring to see the church flourish in the future should first attempt to stay within their present tradition, denomination, or movement and seek ways to bring change from within. The goal is not to start some new group and certainly not to attempt to go out and establish some extreme expression with a cultic following. The first place for discussion is within families as members of families seek to educate and involve one another in change. In the church community, parishioners and leadership need to work together toward a brighter future in an attempt to move thinking beyond the status quo. Even so, sadly, it may be that one may eventually need to join another particular established expression of the church that is better positioned to move the church forward if there appears to be little hope of change within one's original community. Ultimately, it is to be hoped that like-minded communities would come together and identify themselves beyond their present narrow labels. Ultimately, uniting in a more global body that would also allow local expression would certainly be ideal. However, the goal is to not sacrifice purity for the sake of unity.

An agreed-upon, unified standard measure for "purity" must be established. One must adhere to a theistic worldview, understanding that truth is firmly grounded in revelation and not in religion. All authority for what is to be "pure" must begin with this understanding. The Scriptures are God's revelation to humanity and must be understood to be the final and sufficient basis for all that is deemed to be true for living the Christian faith. If any other such authority could have ever existed, there would have been no reason why God would have sought to give us the Scriptures. Furthermore, a corollary to this understanding is that a solid hermeneutic is essential to rightly interpret the Scriptures. And while no interpretation is infallible, a faithful interpretation can certainly be attained.

Again, it must be emphasized that one must begin by adhering to a truly Christian theistic worldview founded upon revelation, not religion. Following this perspective, it must also be acknowledged that a standard must be established as to what truth is and that this truth standard must be the ultimate authority for what is to be the understanding and practice of the Christian faith. As stated above, it is to be argued that the standard for this authority must only be in God's revelation as found in his word, the Holy Scriptures. One cannot serve two masters, both the Scriptures and tradition, with each being equal in authority in determining the Christian faith. In the end, one source will win out. If it is held that a particular interpretation of Scripture found only in one's tradition is the final authority, one would be concluding that the final authority lies with human tradition. It would be more consistent to simply state that the Scriptures are contained in and serve as a part of tradition. Regretfully, this direction in thinking would fall in line with a humanistic worldview rather than a theistic worldview.

If it is determined that Scripture is the final authority, then logically all that is rightfully claimed to be tradition must be consistent with and fall under the authority of the Scriptures. Of course, one might then ask, "How are the Scriptures to be interpreted? Is not tradition needed to do this?" The correct answer is that while tradition is to be considered in the overall interpretation of Scripture, it is Scripture itself that serves as its own final interpreter. In saying this, it is understood that humans and any expression flowing out of humanity (such as that found in tradition) are fallible and may render at best only a "faithful" interpretation. Any human interpretation, whether by a person, group, or council, cannot interpret anything infallibly, where such an interpretation is final and can never be open to question. Only God is infallible. Because God is the source of Scripture, one can conclude that his word (Scripture) is also infallible. Because God is internally consistent, Scripture is also internally consistent and thereby can interpret itself faithfully. Any rightful hermeneutic is based upon this premise.

Thus, the proper hermeneutic to approach the Scriptures would be a theistic hermeneutic rather than a humanistic hermeneutic. In other words, the Scriptures, being "breathed by God" (2 Tim 3:16), are internally consistent, revealing truth as Scripture interprets Scripture. In this, a historical-grammatical understanding that approaches the Scriptures more literally in its natural context is utilized. This averts more humanistic approaches, such as those superimposing a humanly developed theological system onto the Scriptures or those implementing an allegorical, moral, or mystical method of interpretation originating out of the human mind. It is commonly noted, "A text out of context becomes a pretext to a proof text." A theistic approach provides for a "natural" reading easily grasped by a generally educated populace as the word of God is made more readily accessible to the people of God. It is important, therefore, that a particular lens, filter, or grid (e.g. Anglican, Baptist, Roman Catholic, dispensational, Reformed, Presbyterian, Pentecostal, Eastern Orthodox, Methodist, Lutheran, etc.) not be forced upon the Scriptures, whereby the Scriptures are twisted or tweaked to fit a particular persuasion. These lenses, filters, or grids only produce eisegesis, leading to religious humanism and resulting in division within the church.

The following scenario is an example of a humanistic hermeneutic that has become fashionable in recent years. It incorporates the following:

1. Gather humanly acquired extrabiblical information, assuming that this material is related to a biblical account.
2. Assume that this information is sufficiently accurate and complete.
3. Assume that this information is necessary to correctly interpret the account.
4. Project this information onto the biblical account.
5. Assume that this extrabiblical information has influenced the writer and/or the situation (context) of the account.

6. Presume that a correct interpretation of the biblical account can now be attained because of the utilization of this extrabiblical material.

7. Presume that because of the use of this extrabiblical information, the biblical account may, in fact, be isolated and/or localized, thus inferring that the account has little or no relationship to or bearing on other biblical accounts or material.

This humanistic approach is hugely problematic in that it is completely based upon an assumptive/presumptive rationale that demands humanly acquired extrabiblical material as necessary to properly understand a particular biblical account. Rather than first gaining a comprehensive understanding of a matter derived from a thorough study of the whole of Scripture while considering the record of historical interpretation and then discerning the pertinence of any extrabiblical data, this humanistic hermeneutic demands the incorporation of extrabiblical material, relying upon baseless assumptions that may be quite fallacious in the interpretation of a matter. Even more so, such a hermeneutic may be used to completely localize biblical accounts to an extent as to make such accounts completely irrelevant to current application.

Practically speaking, the people of God are to be taught in the Scriptures in such a way as to interpret the Scriptures following a proper hermeneutic. When a matter particular to the Christian faith is discussed, representatives (commonly elders) are chosen by God's people to gather to determine the matter by a faithful interpretation of the Scriptures. A commonly held hermeneutic guides the elders in reaching a conclusion. As previously stated, while this conclusion is not infallible, it may be considered faithful in providing instruction and guidance for God's people. While tradition (such as what is found in commonly held early creeds based on earlier scriptural interpretations) may play an important role in determining a matter, even such aspects of tradition, as important as they are, cannot be considered to be infallible, as only the Scriptures are deemed infallible. Christians, therefore, can live out their faith in confidence while also being open to growing in understanding.

While the realization that no present tradition, denomination, or movement can be touted as the "true" church or contain the full expression of the church, nevertheless, one should not fall into despair, in that much can be learned from each expression. One can find great hope by looking beyond these expressions and seeking a way forward. This way forward must be grounded in a theistic worldview emphasizing God and his revelation (his word) as being sufficient as the final authority for the Christian faith and life, along with a common hermeneutic in interpreting Scripture. After these matters are settled, the early creeds of the church (e.g. Apostles' Creed, Nicene Creed, Athanasian Creed, etc.) and the commonly held propositions found in Christian confessions and catechisms are brought into consideration. From this, a common *kerygma* (proclamation) can best be determined.

What is being suggested is a post-denominational mindset rather than a nondenominational mindset. A nondenominational mindset tends to cast a dim light on past attempts made by traditions, denominations, and movements to find a purer expression of Christianity. A post-denominational mindset seeks to appreciate many of these past attempts while emphasizing that the time has now come to learn from these past expressions and move forward in the Christian faith, becoming more of the church that Christ envisioned. In this endeavor the question may be asked regarding how to protect the church from heresy. While some may maintain that it is these past expressions with their various catechisms, confessions, and hierarchical authority structures that are necessary to protect the church, the historical problem is that many of these past measures of "protection" have all too often gone beyond the Scriptures in propagating their particular perspectives that continue to divide the church. What is needed is a more concise statement that is less contentious and held within a structure that is more organic and less institutional. As previously mentioned, such a statement might be similar to the example found in appendix F.

A Call to Unity, Peace, and Purity

A Portrayal of "Christ's Church"

In recent years it has become apparent that God's people are increasingly seeking authentic community in smaller, more family-type gatherings with a more proactive and consistent spiritual formation. Regretfully, the rise in individualism has left the church with a focus on convenience and consumerism, with superficial mass gatherings led by paid professionals often operating in a top-to-bottom hierarchy, resulting in poor spiritual formation. A return to the more informal relating found in the more bottom-to-top servant-leadership style of the New Testament church is needed. One practical question often asked is, "How can more organic gatherings of Christians take place?" Again, much of the organized church of today has a more or less "top-down" understanding of church. For the most part, this typically focuses on a formal mass gathering on a Sunday morning overseen by paid professionals, propped up by more informal small group gatherings such as a Sunday school or meetings held during the week. Sound familiar? What if the church were depicted more as "bottom-up"? For example, what if small groups led by elders gathered in homes on most Sundays, only meeting in a mass-gathering format on the last Sunday of the month as a culmination of fellowshipping and worshipping more intimately throughout the month? Even such a small change as this would dramatically change the concept of church as we know it.

With the vacuum of mentoring in the lives of so many, an additional plus would be for older people to reinvest in teaching the younger people in the practical living out of the Christian life (Titus 2:1–10). As early as the second century CE until the present day, history records Christianity as becoming increasingly institutional, professional, and heterodox in synthesizing humanistic thinking and culture with biblical truth. However, in the twenty-first century, the tide may be turning. It must be remembered that the church is fundamentally not institutional but is organic in nature. It is a family of God's people based upon a genuine, authentic connection that is more naturally cultivated through time. These connections occur and flourish in relatively small groupings rather than in highly programmed mass gatherings. We must not lose sight of this basic understanding. So, what might the future of his church look like?

An applicable example of uniting a community of those with varying expressions in professing Christ might be as follows: Imagine a township consisting of a thousand inhabitants. Within this township, there are five Christian churches, each claiming to represent a different tradition, denomination, or movement. Suppose that God began to raise up parishioners in each local assembly who became increasingly convinced that God, through his Spirit, was seeking to reclaim his universal church in that township toward greater unity, peace, and purity. While not immediately abandoning their local church, these parishioners begin to meet and discuss how this goal might be accomplished. All parishioners would be united in agreement that while each of their particular churches would have in varying degrees some measure of truthful insight to be contributed, no one church could claim to be the one true expression of the Christian faith. All these participants would hold to a Christian theistic worldview, agreeing that the Scriptures alone are sufficient as the basis of doctrine, and would hold to a common hermeneutic in interpretation. Participants in this ecumenical group would consist of both leaders and non-leaders of their local churches; yet they would agree to hold each other as equals, and each person would have a voice. A primary goal would be to take insights and ideas back to each local church to see if, and to what degree, change might occur in each congregation that would lead to increased unity among the churches. While it would be expected that this would be an ongoing process over some time, nevertheless, the hope would remain that all participants would be continually committed to and invested in the process of glorifying God and becoming the bride of Christ, pleasing in his sight.

One might ask, "Can the church be one while still holding on to particular distinctions?" Yes, of course, as long as these distinctions can be understood and proclaimed as cultural and not doctrinal. As long as the *kerygma* of the Christian faith is understood as supra-cultural and timeless, cultural differences of expression will always be present as people live in ever-changing cultural environments. Some will choose to worship in venues of different architectural designs. Some venues may have pews or chairs, while others will not. Some people may dress one way while others may dress in another way. Music styles will vary. Liturgies or orders of worship may vary. And so on. The main point is that while cultural expressions may vary, these cultural expressions are not to become dogma or be proclaimed obligatory for Christian life and worship. Once such cultural expressions become more than merely cultural expressions, then these expressions become matters depicting religion, not matters depicting revelation. It is important that cultural expressions—buildings, clothes, liturgies, music styles, etc.—not become the focus of what encompasses the Christian faith. If this should happen, these things may easily become idols. While perfection will never be found on this earth, I am convinced that much of the division in the church that exists today can become significantly lessened. This begins with a worldview realignment and a more unified refocusing on the major doctrines solidly proclaimed in Scripture, with less emphasis on issues of minor concern. Ideally, church shepherds will lead the way. If not, then it will come as no surprise if the sheep begin to take matters into their own hands.

Ultimately, by moving forward as has been described, the outcome would be a body of believers representing the *Christian faith* while leaving those who fail to adhere to these basic principles as those representing the *Christian religion*. The great hope is that the people of God will truly seek the heavenly city, the new Jerusalem, in establishing their identity and security in Christ and come to the understanding that the Christian faith lies far beyond Antioch and Alexandria, beyond Rome and Constantinople, beyond Augsburg and Geneva, beyond Zurich and Canterbury, and beyond any earthly city whence the many expressions and traditions holding to Christ have come. We are called by God to find a way toward peace among ourselves rather than division (Ps 34:14; Rom 12:18, 14:17, 19; 1 Cor 14:33; 2 Cor 13:11; Gal 5:22; 1 Thess

5:13; Heb 12:4; Jas 3:17–18; 1 Pet 3:11; 2 Pet 3:14). This manifesto recognizes that all expressions in Christianity—regardless of the particular tradition, denomination, or movement—have, for over two millennia and in varying degrees, been influenced by the humanistic world of religion and philosophy. While we may certainly find valuable aspects within each of our expressions that we may bring to the "peace table," we must be extremely careful not to allow our expressions to cloud our minds and hearts to the point that we abandon the pursuit of Christian peace among ourselves. If this should happen, then our expression will then become an idol and a stumbling block in our lives and, as a result, blind us from finding a way forward. Without question, this would only follow the designs of Satan in causing and maintaining division among God's people. We would tragically be rendering judgment upon ourselves. It is time for God's people to gain a fresh perspective to reclaim the church from the bondage of our humanistic world so that Christ's bride can grow to become more at peace and in unity while striving to attain a greater degree of purity.

The question will arise, "By what name would such a body of believers who hold to the perspective proposed here be called?" Again, it is important to stress that this perspective does *not* suggest starting some new movement, denomination, or tradition. It is *not* advocating anything that would be depicted as some new fringe group or cultic following. While no label can perfectly contain all aspects of this perspective, it may be that this body of believers might simply refer to themselves as "Christ's church." These believers, while temporarily remaining within a particular tradition, denomination, or movement, would, in fact, increasingly realize that their faith transcends all these expressions. While labels may be helpful, the main issue is what is contained under such a label. Again, those of this perspective would hold to a theistic worldview emphasizing God and his revelation (his word) as sufficient as the final authority for the Christian faith rather than the humanistic worldview emphasized within the Christian religion. Those of Christ's church would support the church as being organized and governed by elders as described in the New Testament, serving within a conciliar framework. Finally, it is hoped that such a perspective would seek to reconcile, reclaim, and consolidate the church as one, holy, catholic, and apostolic body of believers.

As has been stated, those who increasingly identify as being of the Christian faith will initially find themselves simultaneously associating with both those of Christ's church as well as those of a particular expression (Baptist, Presbyterian, Catholic, Orthodox, Anglican, etc.). Over time, these particular expressions would become of lesser importance as one's identity in Christ becomes more solidified. Moreover, it is quite likely that these believers will increasingly abandon much of the theological and "churchy" language that has been utilized in the past, especially language that particular traditions, denominations, and movements have utilized, such as "parish," "diocese," "presbytery," "synod," "ordination," "sacrament," "liturgy," "litany," "ordinance," "vestment," etc. For instance, in the English language, instead of using words such as "sacrament" or "ordinance," one might use the word "practice"; instead of "parish," one might use "fellowship"; instead of "ordination," one might use "appointment"; and so forth.

Furthermore, holding extreme positions regarding matters that the Bible does not clearly set forth will become less important. For example, regarding historically contentious theological matters—issues such as baptism or the Lord's Supper—it may be that such believers will come to an agreement that no specific position is spelled out in the Scriptures other than the fact that Christians in the early church regularly participated in the Lord's Supper and that there is one Lord, one faith, and one baptism (Eph 4:5—recognizing that God's people are to be baptized). While properly "discerning the body" in the Lord's Supper is important (1 Cor 11:29), this "discerning" may include some measure of grace in that the body of our Lord will always contain a degree of mystery in the faith (1 Tim 3:9), so there may be room for understandings of the Lord's Supper ranging from a "remembrance" to "real presence." Even baptism may allow both "paedo" (infant) and "credo" (confessional) expressions. Some Christians may even conclude that since there is one Lord (Christ), one faith (in Christ), and one baptism (in Christ), the mode and timing of baptism may not be the most important matter of the Christian faith. As there comes to be increasing agreement in the understanding of one baptism (in Christ), the more common administration may be in both a "consecrational" administration of a believer's child and a "confirmational" administration as one comes to confessional faith. While no doubt there may be those who might remain contentious over such matters, many Christians may finally say "enough" and move on, increasingly finding common ground rather than remaining bogged down in such matters.

Regarding church polity, God's people may organize themselves into local fellowships in neighborhoods, villages, townships, and cities, further expanding into district fellowships, regional fellowships, national fellowships, and even a global fellowship where the unity, peace, and purity of the faith are maintained. Moreover, it is quite plausible that local bodies may decide on an accountability structure that would be more local rather than being accountable to more distant entities. Even so, the primary understanding of the church will be that of an organic rather than a highly institutionalized faith. In time, the concepts of clergy and laity will most likely become less common. Christians in general will become increasingly aware of the importance of all believers becoming better equipped in understanding the faith rather than leaving theological understanding to the "professional Christians." With the growing access to information, more and more people will be able to become theologically self-educated and will become less dependent upon formal academic degrees as proof of their ability to serve the church. Leadership will become more "homegrown" as leaders will be those who have proven themselves over time to be worthy in character, knowledge, wisdom, and experience among the people (1 Tim 3:1–13; Titus 1:5–9). No doubt, some elders may find themselves more intensely involved in their duties than other elders and will need to be relieved of outside vocational responsibilities to better meet the needs of the congregation, thus requiring financial support (1 Tim 5:17–18). Again, this would not be the implementation of a separate clergy class but rather a recognition of those gifted and able to serve in a more focused capacity when conditions allow.

In time, God's people may come to move beyond today's common forms of church polity, such as episcopalism, presbyterianism, or congregationalism, and return to see the church stemming from the biological/spiritual family, as in times past. From early history, it was biological families and those associated with these families that comprised human and spiritual communities. This was also typical of early Christianity. A return to this model would not only provide a more organic, intimate, and spiritually vibrant faith community, but would also return the extended family as the social building block of the church as well as society at large. Elders representing each family-based community would form a conciliar network for governance and accountability for the entire church.

As stated throughout this manifesto, the way forward would first recognize that both philosophy and religion are Satan's counterfeit, stemming from a humanistic worldview that is not only enticing but captivating and even addictive. Again, while this may sound quite naïve and narrow, this understanding is essential. As stated before, those of Christ's church would not strongly self-identify as being of a movement, denomination, or tradition; they would be believers who have come to a perspective that the church is primarily not found in any one institutional formulation but comprises the organic family of God's chosen people. Without question, our present understanding of who we are stems from that which our histories have made us. We cannot change our past. However, who we become will be subject to the future choices that we make. While the Christian may find some temporal association among believers of a particular organizational body, such a one intuitively knows that their basic identity is in Christ, which is paramount and beyond these associations.

As in any shift from a limited position of tunnel vision to becoming able to see beyond and grasp a more promising perspective, groups normally pass through phases in their thinking. Often, this is the same process for Christian traditions, denominations, or movements. Initially, they may begin with (1) believing their group is the only legitimate group and seeing any person who is not part of their group as not truly Christian. Then, while they may still hold their group as the only legitimate group, they may (2) experience an increasing recognition that there are legitimate Christians who are in association with "illegitimate" groups, counting them as wandering or lost sheep in need of returning to the fold (i.e., returning to their particular "legitimate" group). Next, the group may come to the point of making a daring move to (3) actually see that there are, indeed, other legitimate groups; however, they may still hold fast to their group as the "most legitimate." As they are able to move beyond the tunnel, they are then finally able to (4) see other groups as actually legitimate, each having their own positive and negative aspects. Interaction between these groups and between individual Christians can become more trusting and intimate as they count one another as equals in working through their differences. Finally, trust is sufficiently developed to the point that they can (5) proceed in finding increasing doctrinal purity, peace, and unity while recognizing that uniformity in cultural expression may not have to be necessary to allow for such differences.

As our Lord matures his church in the coming years, Christians will no doubt become more able to move beyond a worldly "institutional" understanding to a more organic understanding of the body of Christ, seeing the church as truly a family—an institution with a small "i" in the sense of being institutionally organized and accountable. Christians can then discover increasing freedom from the past institutional notion of what it means to follow Christ in finding their identity and security in a person rather than in a system. Within the Christian family, there is intimacy and trust where the terms of brother and sister, father and mother, as well as uncle and aunt have real meaning. These kinds of relationships are better fostered in smaller groupings as their main relational core. This does not mean that mass gatherings from time to time cannot be beneficial, as all the family can be encouraged to observe numerical growth. However, common sense reminds us that people can only maintain a limited number of meaningful relationships. It is interesting to note that some social scientists, such as Robin

Dunbar, an anthropologist at Oxford University, have concluded that the human brain can only handle around 150 people in their social sphere.[18] Utilizing mass meetings as the common means of relating as a church will only weaken both family and faith. The church cannot afford to drift into a shallow and superficial existence if she is to confront an increasingly godless world. May we learn from history and arise to gird our loins to stand more solidly strong and not remain to wallow in the present morass of apathy and division. We must always keep Christ's severe warning before us that neither a house nor a kingdom divided against itself can stand (Matt 12:25; Mark 3:24–25).

Meanwhile at the Millennial Pub

Some may wonder what the early apostles would think if they walked the streets in today's post-Christian society. Without a doubt, amazement would fill their minds. One can just imagine the apostles strolling into what might be called the Millennial Pub. The pub would primarily be filled with nonbelievers sitting at the bar ordering drink after drink, soaking in the loud music and hanging about with their contemporaries in the main gathering area of the pub. However, in various corners would be the "cool Christians" with their like-minded, theologically astute buddies. In one corner would be the "Young, Restless, and Reformed" bunch; in an opposing corner would be the "Completely Confirmed Catholic"; while in another select corner would be the "Thoroughly Original Orthodox." Yes, characteristically there would be a sprinkling of others: the "ever-lively Pente-Charismatics," the "staunchly cautious Baptists," the "socially minded Methodists," the "posh Anglicans," among many others. Each would have their particular axe to grind, staring one another down, waiting for a theological brawl to break out—everyone enjoys a good fight at the local pub.

In the meantime, the pagans among them would keep scratching their heads, thinking to themselves what a bunch of losers these Christians are who seemingly cannot get their act together, each side filled with pride and smugness, remaining oblivious to what is happening. "Why can't they just get over themselves and maybe make a real difference?" Of course, what everyone at the pub would not realize is that Satan is the bartender who keeps pouring the drinks with glee, secretly relishing in his clueless clientele. If these Christians would only spend as much time and energy seeking the truth that is beyond their traditions, denominations, or movements as they do holding on for dear life defending these expressions, the church could find a more promising way forward. Regrettably, too many Christians are continually deceived into placing their hope and security in the wrong places rather than in God alone. When doing so, their particular perspective or expression becomes an idol.

The apostles would quietly make their way over to a few tacky scattered chairs at the back where the "nobodies" huddle. Yes, these would indeed be the cheap seats. What would cross their minds is anyone's guess. Maybe they would be saddened by the whole scene. Maybe they would be angry. Maybe they would be thinking that they should at least stand up and say something. But maybe they should leave it to these "Christian types" to learn to grow up and take their fight outside and seek to find real unity, peace, and purity for the glory of Christ. Or maybe the apostles might even wonder why God does not just build another ark and do away with the whole lot! (Ah, yes, that rainbow promise thing. Okay. Not an option.). After an hour or so the apostles would pay up and leave the establishment. As they fade into the darkness, one could hear a faint voice among them uttering a prayer ending with "Come, Lord Jesus!" (Rev 22:20). Indeed.

A Final Warning

When reflecting on the words of Jesus, some passages of Scripture have without question left many of us a bit unnerved. One such passage is found in Matt 7:21–23, when Jesus proclaims that not everyone who seemingly does religious acts in Jesus's name is of him. Instead, Jesus declares, "I never knew you; depart from me, you workers of lawlessness." Likewise, there is the passage referring to Jesus cursing a fig tree (Matt 21:18–22; Mark 11:12–14, 20–25), where Jesus compares what had become the empty religious rituals of Judaism to that which is not representative of the true faith.

Such passages should continue to be a reminder to all who consider themselves "religious" Christians: that they may be deceiving themselves regarding the true Christian faith. The apostle Paul reminds us that we need to examine ourselves to see whether we are truly of the faith (2 Cor 13:5). It is to be remembered that it is not merely the outward appearance of things that are of chief concern, it is what lies in the heart of a person that is important to God (1 Sam 16:6–7; 2 Cor 5:11–12). Again, how one views the credibility and sufficiency of God's word is paramount. Those who tend to view the Scriptures as neither being reliable nor credible often tend to drift toward liberalism, while those who tend to view the Scriptures as not being fully sufficient as the basis for Christian faith and life tend to drift toward legalism. Both tendencies have historically led the church into varying influences of humanism that have evolved into the particular traditions, denominations, and movements we are faced with today.

Throughout history, religionists have continually plagued God's people, both before and after the advent of Christ. It is the religionist who establishes doctrines and practices in the name of their religious institution, claiming these to be as authoritative as the very word of God. It is no wonder that increasing numbers of Christians suspiciously hold the established institutional church at a distance, in that most denominations, traditions, and movements are seen as far more interested in the preservation and perpetuation of their expression than in moving forward in the hope of unifying God's people. However, once the tide begins to turn against what has become a highly institutional, professional, and heterodox expression of Christianity—merely a religion among many other religions—a remnant of God's people will emerge seeking to return the Christian faith to its roots. After so many centuries of decay, it may be likely that it will take a transition period of at least three to five generations for a solid body of those holding to the Christian faith to become distinguished from those of the Christian religion as being normative in society. As this development proceeds, it will increasingly be more apparent that it is the Christian religion that divides the church, while it is the Christian faith that unites the church.

Even so, our Lord is calling his people to unity, peace, and purity in the one true faith that he has so graciously revealed to us. Failing to take this matter seriously by just continuing to propagate our particular expression at the expense of all else is more than a minor oversight; it is an act of direct disobedience to his call on our lives. May we not simply ignore or walk away from this call as being unimportant or inconvenient. The future of the spiritual health of his people is at stake as well as the witness of his church before the world. If we truly love our Lord as we say that we do, we need to act by his revealed will without delay (John 14:15, 21; 15:10).

It is important to understand that the faith of God's people began in the garden of Eden and continues to this present day. It is not something that is derived from human culture, nor is it a product of human thought, such as philosophy or religion. The faith of God's people is grounded in God alone and is revealed supernaturally from God himself. Its essence is not merely found in an experience or expressed through some ritualistic activity. It is more than a set of beliefs or doctrines to be argued or to be settled through an apologetic exercise. The faith of God's people is reality itself. It is the very air that is breathed by the believer. One must literally be "born again" into this new reality (John 3:3, 7; 1 Pet 1:3, 23) and become a new creation (2 Cor 5:17; Gal 6:15).

It must always be remembered that from the very beginning, God spoke—he communicates and divinely reveals himself: "In the beginning, God . . . and God said" (Gen 1:1–3). "In the beginning was the Word, and the Word was with God, and the Word was God" (John 1:1). He is the Logos. Since the beginning, God has revealed himself propositionally and ultimately in human flesh. This is why divine revelation (the Scriptures and Christ) is fundamental to the faith and why any human idea and even natural revelation are subject to it. To shift this faith from the foundation of theism to that of humanism is a serious matter that changes the very substance from which this faith is derived. Tragically, through the years, as the church has increasingly succumbed to the deception of humanism, God's people have been fed the counterfeit of religion.

Endnotes

1. Cottret, *Calvin*, 239 (citing John Calvin's 1565 *Leçons ou commentaires et expositions sur les Revelations du prophete Jeremie*).
2. Merriam-Webster, "Revelation."
3. Cambridge English Dictionary, "Philosophy."
4. Merriam-Webster, "Religion."
5. Encyclopaedia Britannica, "Religion."
6. See Barth, *On Religion: The Revelation of God as the Sublimation of Religion*. This is a new translation of §17 of Karl Barth's *Church Dogmatics*, 1/2.
7. Marx, *Critique*, 131.
8. Quoted in "Why the Church Fathers."
9. Quoted in "Why the Church Fathers."
10. Quoted in "Why the Church Fathers."
11. Quoted in "Why the Church Fathers."
12. Quoted in Francoeur, "Why Do Many."
13. Quoted in "Why the Church Fathers."
14. Quoted in Tarico, "20 Vile Quotes."
15. Quoted in "Why the Church Fathers." Brackets and parentheses, and all content contained therein, are represented here as they appear in the source.
16. Wikipedia, "Nuclear Family."
17. Wilberforce, *Real Christianity*, 19–20.
18. Dunbar, "Can the Internet."

Concluding Remarks

The Christian Faith Vs. the Christian Religion

THIS MANIFESTO WOULD LIKE to conclude by emphasizing that the battle for the future of the church lies in understanding the past, present, and continuing influence of religious humanism. Again, this is a worldview issue that will not go away. It is essentially the garden problem reoccurring over and over. While certainly all of God's people each day face the dilemma of whether "God will be God" or whether "I will be God" in their life choices, we can only agree with Jesus in laying the primary blame squarely at the feet of those who serve in places of leadership. Again, it was against the leadership of God's people in his day that Jesus targeted his greatest anger. It was a leadership that continually justified itself by continually holding to traditions that legitimized its authority in pressing the people into obedience, threatening them with the notion that if people opposed them or their theological interpretations, they would be opposing God himself.

We must never forget that "religion" is Satan's counterfeit, continually trying to find a footing in the church whenever and wherever it can. Religion is relentless because it feeds our carnal hearts with deception at every corner. It is a roaring lion seeking to devour us by turning us away from the haven of truth. It comes to us as a wolf in sheep's clothing, speaking lie after lie. Truth always

Concluding Remarks

trumps religious tradition in that the only valid theological tradition of God's people is that which is solidly grounded in the truth of God's word. This is the only legitimate apostolic tradition that can truly be called "sacred."

Satan seeks to cause disunity and alienation in the church, beginning with the Christian family. Let parents never forget that the chief reason for having children is to raise "godly offspring" (Mal 2:15) in the "discipline and instruction of the Lord" (Eph 6:4), carrying the hope that when they are old their children will not depart from how they were raised (Prov 22:6). Let us pray that we heed the words of the prophet Malachi that the hearts of fathers will turn to their children and the hearts of children will turn to their fathers (Mal 4:6), who have sought to remain true and raise their children in the Christian faith. If this does not happen, as was foretold, destruction will certainly follow.

As my thoughts come to a close, somehow I would like to believe that there are enough followers of Christ still out there somewhere who would have the courage to join together to make a real difference toward finding true unity, peace, and purity among ourselves with hearts of humility before God and one another by praying and seeking his face, turning from our sin of division, and asking for forgiveness and the healing of his church. May we be instruments of his peace, remembering that "blessed are the peacemakers, for they shall be called the sons of God" (Matt 5:9).

... that they may all be one.

—*JOHN 17:21*

Epilogue

SPANNING THE PAST MILLENNIA, the battle continues to rage between good and evil, between truth and falsehood, between life and death—ultimately, between God and Satan. As one more clearly understands the history of God's people, parallels become more evident between the history of God's people before the advent of Christ and the history of God's people afterwards. During the time of the old covenant, God divinely spoke to his people regarding the faith. The faith was presented in a form very concretely and tangibly as a foreshadowing of the eternal aspects of the faith as was later revealed in the new covenant. The New Testament letter to the Hebrews discusses this matter.

Even though God's people before the advent of Christ started well in closely adhering to the divine revelation of God in his word; as time passed, the people of God turned the faith of the Jewish people into a religion, eventually adding their ideas as equally authoritative as God's revelation, resulting in Judaism. After the advent of Christ, God's people again began well in adhering to the Scriptures as completely sufficient in understanding the faith and how it is to be lived out. Yet, with time, the Christian faith began to drift as God's people sought to make this faith into a Christian religion as people increasingly believed either that the Scriptures were not completely sufficient or that the Scriptures were not reliable in determining the content of the Christian faith. Again,

Epilogue

God's people turned to their own ideas as being as authoritative as God's revelation.

To begin to understand why the church has come to a place of disunity, lacking peace, and holding to various degrees of purity, one must come to grips with four important elements in this development. The first is the tendency throughout the history of God's people to drift toward the world and its influences. This is the carnal nature of man resulting from the curse of the fall. The second element is the garden problem, resulting in a choice between two opposing worldviews: that of humanism and that of theism. The third element is the awareness of satanic activity within the church and the continual spiritual battle that Christians face. It is Satan's deceptive ways that have continually sought to divide God's people. Finally, human pride blinds God's people from seeing past themselves and their traditions, denominations, or movements, preventing them from moving beyond the present and pressing toward a more promising future.

A practical way of seeing the dilemma before us is to understand that various traditions, denominations, or movements find themselves somewhere on a spectrum representing a rather simple organic Christian faith underpinned by theism at one end and a highly institutionalized Christian religion underpinned by humanism at the opposing end. Consequently, those of us who identify with one of these expressions are likewise caught along this spectrum, trying to make sense of it all.

It is the ardent prayer of God's people to increasingly cry out for a way forward beyond the forces that have so long divided the bride of Christ. May we be bold enough to risk confronting the institutionalized church, the usual culprit in resisting change, with the challenge of being able to see beyond the fortress walls of the present and creatively gain a glimpse of the larger future landscape for the glory of our Lord. Surely, it has become evident that the status quo is no longer viable.

Appendix A

Criticisms

THE FOLLOWING IS AN attempt to address the three most common criticisms that readers may have regarding the basic content of this manifesto.

1. *The premise of this manifesto is that if Christians would simply adopt the goal of ridding the church of religion, then the possibility of the church becoming a people purer, more unified, and more at peace might become a greater reality. This appears to be far too naïve and simplistic, even if Christians could ever agree upon such a goal. Furthermore, finding any common agreement regarding what is considered to be religion would be impossible.*

When a person derides religion in the church it can often be seen as coming from someone who is quite narrow or fundamentalist in their perspective. However, when one understands that religion is a product of a humanistic worldview, the conversation soon changes. The discussion then becomes about one's definition of humanism. As one comes to understand that a humanistic worldview stems from humanity's efforts to set humanity, or proclamations originating from humans, as authoritative—either equal, above, or contrary to God or his proclamations—then one discovers that this perspective is in direct opposition to a true understanding of a theistic worldview. This conflict began in the

Appendix A

garden of Eden and continues today. It is from this understanding that dialogue and critique of what has transpired within church history can find promise. While many may be quick to find fault and inadequacies in any proposal to help the church become what Christ has desired his church to be, often no better proposal is offered.

> 2. *This manifesto contends that there are only two worldviews (humanism and theism) from which people live out their lives. Holding to only a two-worldview option appears far too limited compared to what most people would adhere to.*

No doubt most of us who have given much thought to the concept of worldview have been schooled to think in terms of numerous worldviews. What is often described in the literature as a worldview would better be described as a "paradigm" or an "archetype." This manifesto comes out of the theistic understanding that God has revealed to us the true perspective of how we are to see the world around us. This understanding embraces the events of what historically took place in the garden of Eden, the beginning of human existence. God's word describes man's basic dilemma as that which seeks either: 1) God as God and the ultimate source of all that is true, or, in some way, 2) man as God or man possessing the ability to act as God. Since most people are not truly theistic in their thinking, they must then rely on sources other than God's revelation found in the Scriptures as their fundamental approach to life. They see the Scriptures as irrelevant, unreliable, or insufficient.

> 3. *What this manifesto proposes is a reclamation so radical and discomforting that church leaders would never allow their people to follow such a direction. There is too much at stake to risk changing the status quo, especially if these leaders would have to admit that any aspect of their tradition, denomination, or movement might be leading their people astray.*

Duly noted. Seeking such a reclamation is indeed daunting and not for the fainthearted. However, just continuing the status

Appendix A

quo by retreating to our theological and/or ecclesiastical corner gives little hope for God's people who are yearning for the body of Christ to come together as his bride in unity, peace, and purity. The underlying question that needs to be answered is, who or what is preventing this from happening? As in the day of our incarnated Lord on this earth, it seems to always come back to the religious leaders. Somehow leaders protecting their turf or clinging to power by manipulating the situation in their favor appears to be the primary means by which such leaders keep things "as is."

By such behavior, the people in the pews are being neglected at best, or, at worst, being abused. Then again, perhaps such a conclusion is too harsh. More than likely, it is simply the cowardice or laziness on the part of leaders that leaves the saints hopeless and demoralized. As long as Christians habitually just go through the motions while not upsetting anyone, why should we care? As in the C. S. Lewis classic *The Screwtape Letters*, Satan seeks to deceive God's people through fear, busyness, or indifference, or by other means to tempt the saint to divest himself or herself of the most important things in living as God intends. However, just blaming the church leadership will not necessarily get anywhere. We cannot just blame others. We must stand before God individually and give an account of ourselves. Even so, as in times past, it is often the common people who may have to wake up the leaders to act. Quite frankly, when people start voting with their feet and with their pocketbooks, church leaders will be forced to rise to the occasion. I, myself, as a church leader need to take heed.

Appendix B

Common Depictions of Christianity

The most accurate depiction of Christianity may be described as the *Christian faith*. This is simply the understanding of Christianity as that held by the apostles and first-century Christians. This faith was initially called "the Way" (Acts 9:2; 19:9) following Jesus's description of himself as "the way, and the truth, and the life." (John 14:6). It held to God's revelation of himself in Christ and in the Scriptures. The Scriptures were the affirmed Hebrew Scriptures (the Masoretic Text) and the completed first-century writings of the apostles and those associated with them in what is called the New Testament. The Hebrew Scriptures were not based upon the Septuagint, the Greek version of the Old Testament, which included other writings often referred to as the "deutero-canonical" or "duo-canonical" writings or the "Apocrypha." This does not mean that the writers of the New Testament did not cite passages from the Septuagint (as they did), but they did so as this text was already in the Greek language. To those of the Christian faith, divine revelation as contained in the Masoretic Text and in the New Testament represented God's propositional revelation.

As has been mentioned in this manifesto, much of the current view of Christianity is that of the *Christian religion*. This depiction represents some of the underpinnings of the *Christian faith* that have been syncretized with man's ideas to varying degrees throughout the past centuries. Regretfully, some of these

Appendix B

expressions of the Christian religion have even gone as far as to have adopted humanism as the basis of their expressions, resulting in a Christianized religious humanism. It is this Christian religion that depicts a counterfeit form of the true faith that has captivated the hearts and lives of so many of those who call themselves Christian. It is the focus of this manifesto to call Christians to move beyond the Christian religion and embrace the Christian faith.

Finally, some find themselves in what might be called the *Christian culture*. This involves elements of a particular culture that have been influenced by Christianity. These cultural expressions may be in art, music, architecture, literature, customs, etc., and may be relatively harmless unless these elements become obligatory for living the Christian life or become the focus of a Christian's attention. Sadly, some expressions of Christianity may embrace such cultural elements to the point of leading one to believe that they must also embrace such elements to be a true Christian. Such a situation leads to legalism. Also, there is the danger of a person believing that just because they embrace these Christianized elements, this alone would be sufficient to make them a Christian.

Appendix C

Thinking Outside the Box

OFTEN, WE ARE ONLY able to see things in a certain way. For example, draw four dots on a piece of paper in a way that connecting the dots would form a box. If instructions are given that all the dots are to be connected without lifting the pencil or pen, and without retracing any lines, most of us would say that this would be impossible. If one starts in one corner and proceeds to connect all the corners, then one would still need to connect the opposing corners. This would require making an X within the box. If one can only imagine doing this while staying within the box, then the task would look undoable. However, if one was able to think "outside the box" by making a dot outside the box, then connecting the dots in the opposing corners of the box would be possible by connecting one of the corners to the outside dot and then continuing to connect this outside dot to the corner horizontal to the original corner and then to the final opposing corner, making an X.

The reason for demonstrating the "box problem" is to remind us that often we see problems only in a certain way, such as seeing possible solutions only within the "box," or how we have normally seen things. Often by approaching problems only by staying within the box, we may find ourselves limited in seeing possible solutions. However, by being able to see outside the box, we can more easily discover solutions.

Appendix C

When trying to solve theological differences, we sometimes find ourselves at an impasse because we are only able to see things in a certain way. Sometimes perceived theological differences appear to be impossible to reconcile. As a result of not being able to see outside the box of our thinking, these differences may continue, even for centuries.

The challenge of this manifesto is to ask all of God's people to become more able to see our theological differences beyond the boxes that have limited our thinking in the past and strive to see a possible "third way" forward that would better reconcile what we have previously perceived as impossible to reconcile. For example, when attempting to reconcile parties in conflict who seemingly can only think of solutions as either A or B, one of the tasks of a mediator is to get the parties to come up with a possible C or D solution that they have not yet been able to imagine. Only by doing so can they find a possible way forward.

As God's people, it is our future hope that we will be able to better see through God's eyes rather than our own eyes, and possibly find solutions outside the box of our imaginations so that unity, peace, and purity can have a chance. On the other hand, regretfully, some people seriously believe that it is their life's mandate to try to "figure everything out" or to be able to answer every question. Some Christians, often described as apologists, even fall into this trap. It is important to understand that God is simply too big and his ways too unknowable to ever be fully explained (Isa 55:8–9). We are reminded that "of making of many books there is no end" (Eccl 12:12), and we are warned that there will be those who are "always learning and never able to arrive at the knowledge of the truth" (2 Tim 3:25). This is not an argument against gaining knowledge but the simple reminder that man's knowledge has limitations.

Appendix D

The Concept of a "Multiverse"

VERY OFTEN WHEN ONE envisions concepts such as heaven or hell, there may tend to be some notion of a physical place existing at some particular time. From a child's perspective, there is a common understanding of heaven as a place beyond the clouds or of hell as abiding deep within the earth's core. The idea of an existence, a world, or a universe beyond our understanding of time and space is, without a doubt, a difficult reality that seems beyond comprehension. However, the Scriptures tend to indicate that such a reality indeed exists. An eternal "other universe," outside time and space, where God and created beings such as angels and demons reside, is plainly stated within the biblical narrative. The question is, "How does such a universe relate to the present created universe in which we live?"

In the New Testament we are told that, as believers, "even when we were dead in our trespasses, [God] made us alive together with Christ—by grace you have been saved—and raised us up with him and seated us with him in the heavenly places in Christ Jesus" (Eph 2:5–6). In Col 1:1–3 we are again reminded, "If then you have been raised with Christ, seek the things that are above, where Christ is seated at the right hand of God. Set your mind on things that are above, not on things that are on earth. For you have died, and your life is hidden with Christ in God." Verses such as these indicate that the life of the Christian is essentially beyond

Appendix D

this present universe. It has sometimes been said by theologians that one must first leave this world to live in this world; or it may be quipped that "a man of God must have his head in the heavens and his feet on the ground . . . and there is a lot of stretching in between!"

In today's world of scientific investigation, the notion of parallel universes or a "multiverse" has now become a daily discourse. Early in the twentieth century, Einstein rejected Newton's commonly held notion of absolute time. For Einstein, time was somewhat like a fluid, going everywhere rather than being chronologically linear with a sense of past, present, and future. Furthermore, space and time were seen to be inextricably connected. Even as early as Plato and Aristotle, philosophical thinking debated reality as being either of this world or of a world beyond. Much later in history, even stories such as *The Lord of the Rings* and *The Chronicles of Narnia* tell of fantasy worlds such as Middle Earth and Narnia that have entertained the minds of both children and adults alike with the concept of a realm beyond the one in which we live. Theoretical notions such as the "God particle" and popular movies like *Tomorrowland*, *Interstellar*, and *The Theory of Everything* play into this idea.

In the Scriptures, we find glimpses into God's realm. Early in Genesis, God is set apart from his creation. As he creates, reference is made to "days" of creation, possibly leading one to interpret that God was creating chronologically according to our notion of days within our universe and the order in which we exist. Sadly, this understanding has led philosophers, theologians, and scientists to endlessly contend throughout history over the issue of how "old" the universe is. A more helpful understanding is that God created the universe from within his realm, without time or space, which is then translated into our realm. Thus, "days" are simply "God days" that no philosopher, theologian, or scientist will ever be able to measure. So, the six days of creation are God days, which are without measure, whether being twenty-four of "our" hours or twenty-four of "our" seconds or twenty-four billion of "our" years. Trying to ever calculate God days is only an exercise in futility. We

Appendix D

must remember that no one was around to observe the phenomenon of creation; only God was there. Furthermore, to talk in terms of "was," "is," or "will be" is nonsense talk in a realm where time does not exist and there is no cause and effect. While a sense of chronology is obviously present in the creation story, where earth needed to previously exist before humanity could be formed, how this chronological story is translated from God's creational decrees will always remain a mystery.

Other well-known examples from the Scriptures noting a heavenly realm are described in the narrative of Job and his dialogue with God; the apostle Paul's vision of a "third heaven"; and the account of heaven recorded by the apostle John in Revelation. The timelessness of Christ is noted in declarations such as "Before Abraham was, I AM" (John 8:58) and "I am the Alpha and Omega, the beginning and the end" (Rev 1:8, 21:6, 22:13). The apostle Peter states that "with the Lord, one day is as a thousand years" (2 Pet 3:8). The more one is able to grasp the perspective of God acting in a realm that is without time or space, many issues debated by theologians become muted.

For instance, the debate over free will versus predestination addressing one's salvation depends upon arguments that infer time and, thus, causation. The Calvinist says that "one believes *because* one is saved" while the Arminian says "one is saved *because* one believes." Molinists have even speculated of a "middle knowledge" of God in order to try to reconcile these notions. However, when causation is removed, all that remains is "those who believe are saved" and "those who are saved believe." End of story. There is no need of one "cooperating" with God in one's salvation and there is no *ordo salutis* (order of salvation). For example, when one reads Rom 8:29–30 ontologically rather than chronologically, concepts such as predestination, calling, justification, and glorification simply coexist rather than depend upon one another. Because salvation resides solely within the purposes of God, who exists beyond time, believing and being saved essentially are not causal in God's realm (although in our realm time, and thus causality, occupy our minds). Holding that God is sovereign in all things does not mean

Appendix D

that people do not truly matter, or that a person's will is immaterial. One must come to the place in understanding that many things will always remain a mystery when contemplating who God is and how he acts. Thus, while one may infer causation when reading the Scriptures, it is important to gain God's perspective as we read. To grasp that God can deal with World War II simultaneously with events in the year 2050 is quite far-reaching to our imaginations. Thus, the idea of a multiverse is one concept that is tremendously helpful as we read the Scriptures and discuss many theological differences. God dwells and acts in a realm (universe) that is not our realm.

Furthermore, from a heavenly perspective, matters that we often see as "either/or" may actually be "both/and." A prime example of a both/and understanding is in the soteriological perceptions of Roman Catholics and Protestants over "infused" righteousness versus the "imputed" righteousness of the believer. As a result, when one has a limited, earthly perspective, one can easily stumble over the concepts of justification and sanctification. A theological contention throughout much of Christian history is in the understanding of "justification" communicated by the apostle Paul in his letter to the Roman believers and that communicated by the apostle James in his letter. Paul seems to state that one is justified by faith without works (Rom 3:20–28), whereas James indicates that without works, faith is dead (Jas 2:17, 24). However, the Scriptures teach that a true saving faith leading to a believer's justification is a faith leading to a transformed/transforming life. Justification, therefore, has both a positional as well as a progressive element. It is the same with sanctification. The author of the letter to the Hebrew believers speaks of saints who "have been sanctified" (a positional state) as well as those who are "being sanctified" (a progressive state) (Heb 10:10–14). Our position in Christ leads to a full assurance of our salvation because the righteous works of his life, death, and resurrection fulfill all the requirements necessary for our salvation. We as believers have the righteousness of God (2 Cor 5:21; Eph 4:23–24; Phil 3:9) although we must still work out this salvation as God works within us (Phil 2:12–13). Assurance of

Appendix D

the believer's salvation lies in Christ's finished work rather than in the efforts of the believer. This, in essence, is the gospel, which is indeed good news!

Appendix E

Community Fellowships of Christ's Church

OVER MUCH OF THE past two thousand years, it is of little question that God's people seem relentless in creating their special "niche" in the Christian world, leading to division after division to the delight of Satan. Maybe it is high time that each local congregation or parish begin to ask themselves challenging questions such as: How much time and effort is our church giving to promote Christian unity, peace, and purity in our community? Is just coming together with other denominations for some local common cause once per year investing seriously in responding to our Lord's prayer to be unified and not divided as his people? How are we mending our theological differences?

While there may be larger movements among leadership, such as the Gospel Coalition among evangelicals or global organizations such as the World Reformed Fellowship, what can be done on the local level among the common folk? What is being proposed is the establishment of community fellowships of Christ's Church. These fellowships would not be a local church or compete with the local church. Rather, these fellowships would be ecumenical extensions of local churches, seeking to bring unity, peace, and purity among fellow believers representing the various churches. These communities would not promote particular theological persuasions or engage in the administration of ordinances or sacraments. Rather these fellowships would target their focus on the study of the Scriptures in gaining a better understanding of the Christian faith. Governance of fellowships would be overseen by those who would meet the biblical qualifications of leaders and ideally represent existing local churches. To ensure orthodoxy, these fellowships would utilize approved resources not representing any particular tradition, denomination, or movement, and facilitators would be trained in the use of such resources. All attempts would be made to provide instruction basic to all who would hold to a truly orthodox, evangelical, and catholic faith. However, as to be expected, churches whose primary focus is to prevent their congregants from being exposed to teachings other than that of their particular persuasion would most certainly oppose such ecumenical gatherings. Regretfully, such churches would most likely be more committed to religion than to the Christian faith. Yet, it is precisely the ridding of God's people from the propaganda of religion that is the way forward to bringing his church to unity, peace, and purity. If the existing local churches fail to respond to the call to reconcile the people of God in the Christian faith, these fellowships may then be left with no other option than to establish their own local churches.

Ideally, fellowships would meet at least a couple of times per month in a casual and intimate environment such as homes or small rented venues. Meetings would involve a time of fellowship, prayer, and study and would normally consist of under thirty people. These community fellowships would focus on the core teachings of the Christian faith rather than on teachings and practices particular to a religious tradition, denomination, or movement that might typically be found in a local church setting. It is hoped that local churches would not see these fellowships as a threat to their existence but rather as an attempt to further the cause of Christian unity, peace, and purity that has been historically elusive and difficult to achieve when dealing with large institutional bodies so often entrenched in maintaining the status quo.

Appendix F

Example of a Statement of Faith[1]

1. We believe in the Triune God, eternal in three distinct persons, Father, Son, and Holy Spirit, one God, the Creator of Heaven and Earth.
2. We believe that the Holy Scriptures of the Old and New Testaments as originally given are the only inspired and infallible record of the revelation of God to humanity and are the supreme authority in all matters of life and faith.
3. We believe in the sovereignty of God in creation, providence, and redemption.
4. We believe God's acts of creation are responsible for the origin of all things seen and unseen, and that creation according to the biblical record is a historical event.
5. We believe that gender is a function of God's created order and that there are only two genders, male and female, as determined biologically. Men and women are equally made in the image of God for distinct roles within the family and the church.
6. We believe marriage is a mutually exclusive relationship between a man and a woman.

---

[1]. Adapted from the statement of faith of the Island-to-Island Gospel Fellowship, of which I am a trustee. Used with permission.

7. We believe in the providence of God whereby he upholds the universe, governs the world, supplies the needs of his creatures, and brings his people to salvation and his will to pass.

8. We believe that humanity, from the moment of conception, was created in the image and likeness of God to have dominion over the earth and to do all things to the glory of God.

9. We believe in humanity's universal fall into sin through Adam's transgression and in humanity's subsequent guilt, depravity, judgment, and condemnation.

10. We believe in Jesus Christ, the only begotten son of the Father; that he was conceived by the Holy Spirit, born of a virgin, crucified as a ransom for many, died and was buried, was bodily resurrected from the dead, and ascended into heaven; and that he is presently at the right hand of God the Father and will personally return to earth in power and glory to judge the living and the dead.

11. We believe in the free offer of salvation to all humanity and the necessity of faith in the Lord Jesus Christ to be saved.

12. We believe that God declares those who trust Christ for salvation to be justified not on account of their own merit but solely because of God's grace.

13. We believe in the necessity of the work of the Holy Spirit to apply the benefits of Christ's redemptive work to individual sinners, working in them regeneration, faith, repentance, sanctification, and glorification.

14. We believe the Holy Spirit's indwelling of the believer begins at regeneration and enables the believer to increasingly die to sin and to live for righteousness.

15. We believe in the bodily resurrection of all humanity, the unjust being raised to everlasting punishment, and the just being raised to everlasting life and being conformed to Christ's glorious body.

Appendix F

16. We believe in one holy universal church, the body of Christ, to which all God's redeemed people belong and in which they are united through the Spirit, and that the church is commissioned to proclaim the gospel of God's salvation in Jesus Christ to all the world.

17. We believe all Christians are to be identified with Christ and his church through water baptism in the name of the Father, the Son, and the Holy Spirit and regularly come together around the Lord's Table to proclaim his death until his return. These sacraments (ordinances/practices) are outward and visible signs of inward and spiritual grace that proclaim the gospel alongside preaching the word of God.

Appendix G

Example of a Post-Denominational Church

IMAGINE A GEOPOLITICAL DISTRICT or county called York. In this district there are several churches, some affiliated with a denomination or tradition as well as churches that are independent and nondenominational. In the midst of this setting are a group of Christians in the district who seek to gather together under the conviction of establishing an ecumenical and post-denominational church in the hope of providing a more consistent witness of Christ's prayer for a more united, pure, and peaceful body of believers. They choose to call this church Trinity Church.

Trinity Church encourages other churches in the district to join them under a common statement of faith in a local district fellowship called York District Christian Faith Churches. This fellowship allows independent nondenominational churches to not exist in isolation, without any fellowship, support, or accountability from other local Christian congregations of similar faith, while encouraging local churches of traditional or denominational affiliation to find a local ecumenical identity and support beyond the confines of their particular persuasion. Congregants of these churches would join together to support cohort group activities within their congregations for men, women, single adults, seniors, youth, and children. In addition, congregants may also find

Appendix G

common local community involvement such as in education, business, local government, recreation, and outreach opportunities.

Many of the congregants of Trinity Church have come out of various denominations or traditions and bring their diverse experiences found in each expression. Other members have very little, if any, church background. Trinity Church is established under the leadership of three to five elders along with three to five deacons. Under this leadership, Trinity Church seeks to incorporate some aspects of former denominations and traditions while holding the historical creeds of the early church in accordance with the Scriptures. In keeping with the goal of promoting intimate community and discipleship, the ideal congregational size would consist of between 75 and 125 congregants. It is hoped that at least one of the elders will have a sense of a particular call to be more vocationally involved in the local church and will have demonstrated abilities in congregational oversight as well as having giftings in the understanding and public communication of God's word. Such a one would seek to gain ongoing biblical and theological development for pastoral ministry. While all of the elders are adequately equipped for teaching and leading the church, the church will recognize this particular elder as their pastor.

In the attempt to maintain an organic family community of believers and not become highly institutional, Trinity Church is established upon the concept of concentrating on small gatherings rather than large mass events. There is little emphasis on "clergy" and "laity." All members are involved in spiritual formation at every age level though ongoing developmental opportunities. These opportunities may include a set curriculum as well as practical application in real-world encounters. All those in teaching/leadership positions undertake biblical and theological training, and all church officers are vetted at an acceptable level of biblical and theological knowledge. In order to promote an intimate church family culture as well as interchurch worship and fellowship, Trinity Church meets publicly in congregational worship on the first and third Sundays of the month and in home assemblies on the second and fourth Sundays of each month. Quarterly, on the

Appendix G

fifth Sunday, Trinity congregants worship at other Christian faith churches of the York district or in a combined church worship. The prayer of Trinity Church is to portray itself as a witness in encouraging all believers in the district to strive to fulfill Christ's prayer for the unity, peace, and purity of his people.

Sample of Sunday Public Worship at Trinity Church

Public Congregational Worship: 10:00–10:45 a.m.

Announcements (pre-worship)

Call to Worship and Psalm
Song
Old Testament reading
Song
New Testament reading
Song
Gospel reading
Children's moment
Pastoral and offertory prayer
Creed/confession
Thanksgiving and congregational prayer/Lord's Prayer
Homily (5–7 minutes)
Communion
Closing song
Benediction

Fellowship/Bible study: 10:45–11:30 a.m.
Fellowship groups with refreshments in classrooms

Appendix G

Notice for Sunday Worship

1st/3rd Sundays:
Public congregational worship: 10:00–10:45 a.m.
Fellowship and Bible study: 10:45–11:30 a.m.

2nd/4th Sundays:
Local home assemblies: 10:00–11:30 a.m.

Quarterly 5th Sundays:
Public worship at other local churches, or combined worship

Appendix H

Establishing a Post-Denominational Church

- Pray—about how you might be involved in trying to fulfill our Lord's prayer stated in John 17. Pray that others will grasp this vision.
- Share—this vision with other local believers, especially with the leadership in your church.
- Assess—how supportive your church leadership is regarding this vision.
  - Would the leadership consider your church becoming a post-denominational church? If so, how would this occur?
  - Would your church be supportive of the establishment of a local post-denominational church? If so, reassure the church leadership that such a church would intend on being in an association with other like-minded churches that would provide mutual fellowship, support, and accountability.
- Propose—a post-denominational church that would adopt:
  - A priority of promoting doctrinal purity as well as peace and unity among Christ's church.

Appendix H

- A priority of small over large gatherings in a local community.
  - Local church total of 75–125 adherents
  - House groups of 12–25 adherents
  - Small groups of 6–12 adherents
- Leadership without clericalism.
  - 3–5 elders
  - 3–5 deacons
- Formal and informal gatherings.
  - More formal public gatherings
  - More informal home and small group gatherings
- Fellowship, support, and accountability with other local churches.
  - Encourage regular visitation of other local churches
  - Encourage joint church gatherings
  - Encourage joint church outreach and missions
  - Encourage joint church discipleship opportunities
  - Encourage joint cohort groups with other local churches: men, women, children, youth, young adult singles, seniors, etc.

Bibliography

Augustine. *On the Spirit and the Letter.* Translated by Peter Holmes. Logos Virtual Library. https://www.logoslibrary.org/augustine/spirit/.

Barth, Karl. *On Religion: The Revelation of God as the Sublimation of Religion.* Translated by Garrett Green. London: T&T Clark, 2006.

Cambridge English Dictionary. "Philosophy." https://dictionary.cambridge.org/us/dictionary/english/philosophy.

Cottret, Bernard. *Calvin: A Biography.* London: A & C Black: 2003.

Dunbar, Robin. "Can the Internet Buy You More Friends?" TEDx Talks, March 2012. youtube.com/watch?v=o7IpED729k8&feature=youtu.be.

Encyclopaedia Britannica. "Religion." https://www.britannica.com/topic/religion.

Marx, Karl. *Critique of Hegel's "Philosophy of Right."* Edited by Joseph O'Malley. Translated by Annette Jolin and Joseph O'Malley. Cambridge: Cambridge University Press, 1982. Google Books. https://books.google.com/books?id=uxg4AAAAIAAJ.

Merriam-Webster. "Religion." https://www.merriam-webster.com/dictionary/religion.

———. "Revelation." https://merriam-webster.com/dictionary/revelation.

The Nicene Creed. https://www.creeds.net/ancient/nicene.htm.

Tarico, Valerie. "20 Vile Quotes Against Women By Religious Leaders From St. Augustine to Pat Robertson." *AlterNet*, June 30, 2013. https://www.alternet.org/2013/06/20-vile-quotes-against-women-religious-leaders-st-augustine-pat-robertson.

"Why the Church Fathers Were So Negative About Sex." Nov. 1, 2007. https://whychurchfatherswerenegativeaboutsex.blogspot.com.

Wilberforce, William. *Real Christianity: A Practical View of the Prevailing Religious System of Professed Christians in the Higher and Middle Classes in This Country, Contrasted with Real Christianity.* 1797. Revised and updated by Bob Beltz. Ventura, CA: Regal, 2006.

Bibliography

Wikipedia. "In necessariis unitas, in dubiis libertas, in omnibus caritas." https://en.wikipedia.org/wiki/In_necessariis_unitas,_in_dubiis_libertas,_in_omnibus_caritas.
———. "Nuclear Family." https://en.wikipedia.org/wiki/Nuclear_family.

www.ingramcontent.com/pod-product-compliance
Lightning Source LLC
Chambersburg PA
CBHW071443160426
43195CB00013B/2015